Mme Theresa,
Thank you so much for all our help
and for always being a to be
around

Love
Tiatsi

Mr
WAS
HERE WITH US. GOOD LUCK
SISSJ
Thembanhare,
Dryeld, mother,
Mmscather

The
abduction and trial
of Jestina Mukoko

Mme Therese
thank you so much for
all your hard work, please come
again
Andrew Matagaty

AUNTIE THERESA;
Thank you
no, no, no, no
much for your
support — it
was invaluable —
shall look forward
to continued conversations! dearly

It was good
working with you
Auty Theresa,
you will be missed

You have
been a star
safe trip
Kibo

Ahi

The abduction and trial of Jestina Mukoko

THE FIGHT FOR HUMAN RIGHTS IN ZIMBABWE

Jestina Mukoko

KMM

Review
Publishing

Published in 2016
KMM Review Publishing Company (PTY) Ltd
PO Box 782114, Sandton 2146
Website: www.kmmr.co.za

ISBN 978-0-9922329-5-5

Typesetting and layout: Brandon van Heerden.
Printing and binding: Colors, Johannesburg.

CONTENTS

Acknowledgements

I dedicate this book to my son, Takudzwa, my siblings, both living and departed, and my mother, *mbuya* Mukoko, for their show of great love, sacrifice and selflessness. Not forgetting my nephew, Vincent Mapiye, for the courage and words of wisdom that echo in my ears.

My most profound and heartfelt gratitude extends to the Zimbabwe Lawyers for Human Rights for their dedication, commitment and unwavering support:

Irene Petras
Otto Saki
Roselyn Hanzi
Dzimbabwe Chimbga
Beatrice Mtetwa
Harrison Nkomo
Alec Muchadehama
Andrew Makoni

Foreword

Jestina Mukoko, the Director of the Zimbabwe Peace Project, a primary documentation institution, was abducted from her home in Norton, about 31 km from Harare, today, Wednesday 3 December, around 05h00 by armed plain clothed security agents believed to be the Central Intelligence Organisation (CIO).

When I read the Zimbabwe Peace Project news alert at 7h00 on 3 December 2008 I felt as though I had received a physical blow. My knees turned to water. If I had not been sitting down, I would have collapsed. I found it particularly chilling that Jestina had been taken away in her nightdress. I was still in my nightdress myself, having gone from my bed straight to my computer, anxious to start follow-up work on protest action I was helping to organise as part of the annual campaign, 16 Days of Activism for No Violence against Women and Children.

I had met Jestina Mukoko in Tanzania in 2008 when we were both members of a Zimbabwean civil society delegation to Dar es Salaam for a series of meetings with our Tanzanian counterparts. Jestina did not strike me as particularly friendly and she was not someone one would notice in a crowd. But when she took the podium and spoke, I sat up and listened. With her perfect broadcaster's diction, she outlined the work of the network of Zimbabwe Peace Project monitors at local level in Zimbabwe.

By the time she finished she had the audience, including me, in the palm of her hand. My overwhelming impression was one of strength, courage and consistency. That impression was reinforced by later meetings and I was delighted when the Zimbabwe Peace Project won the Crisis in Zimbabwe Coalition Human Rights award in 2009.

'Who has died?' asked my housekeeper, who had come running from the kitchen in response to my cry of alarm. I could barely talk. In my mind,

Jestina was as good as dead. I recalled with horror the abduction of Abigail Chiroto the day after her husband, Emmanuel Chiroto, a councillor for the opposition Movement for Democratic Change (MDC), was elected mayor of Harare. On 16 June 2008 a group of men, some wearing military uniform, had firebombed the Chiroto's home and abducted Abigail and their four-year-old son, Ashley. The attackers drove off in two double-cab vehicles with no number plates. Ashley was dropped off at a police station but there was no sign of Abigail until her brutalised body was found on 18 June.

Abigail was not the only one. MDC activist Tonderai Ndira was also abducted in June 2008, his body discovered two weeks later. In 2007 freelance cameraman Edward Chikomba suffered the same fate. In 2000 MDC official Patrick Nabanyama disappeared, never to be seen again. Would Jestina suffer the same fate: I wondered, as I tried to control my feelings of panic and grief.

A call from my colleague Nixon Nyikadzino calmed me down and brought home the fact that there was no time for panic or hysteria, there was work to be done. He had been on the phone to Harare and he briefed me on how human rights and civic organisations had swung into action to try to locate Jestina. As the head of the South African office of the Crisis in Zimbabwe Coalition, I was expected to lead the response, alerting the regional and international community about Jestina's abduction.

That morning, Nixon and I sent dozens of emails to anyone and everyone we knew – media, church and women's organisations, the South African High Commission in Zimbabwe, the African National Congress (ANC) and South African human rights organisations, regional organisations and our solidarity networks within the region. The gist of the messages was: 'We fear for Jestina's life. The more widely the information is circulated the greater the possibility of her release. Please pass the word around.' We urged people to call the then Zimbabwean ambassador to South Africa, Simon Khaya Moyo, to demand information about Jestina's whereabouts.

At lunchtime I took food to a group of young women refugees who were picketing in Church Street, near the Union Buildings in Pretoria, in protest against violence against and the abuse of women in Zimbabwe. The women reacted emotionally to the news of Jestina's abduction and vowed to step up their protest action. I had a hasty consultation with activist Sox Chikhowero and other organisers of the protest to realign the protest to focus on Jestina's abduction. We agreed that the first step was to issue a press statement.

By the time I got back home to draft the press statement there was more news from Harare and it was not good. The Crisis Coalition's online Daily Catalyst of 3 December reported that at 10.30am the Bulawayo offices of Zimbabwe Lawyers for Human Rights (ZLHR) had been raided by riot police armed with AK47 machine guns, revolvers and batons. The police accused ZLHR of harbouring members of the Zimbabwe Congress of Trade Unions (ZCTU).

At 11h05 ZCTU Secretary-General, Wellington Chibhebhe, and other ZCTU leaders as well as Crisis Coalition spokesperson Japhet Moyo were arrested as they were addressing workers, reporting back on a meeting they had held with Reserve Bank Governor Gideon Gono to discuss the havoc that severe limitations on daily cash withdrawals were wreaking on the lives of workers. By 1pm, more than 70 demonstrators had been arrested countrywide and five women were receiving medical attention after being beaten by the police.

It was clear that the abduction of Jestina Mukoko was not an isolated incident but part of a renewed campaign of state-sponsored violence and repression. That afternoon the Crisis in Zimbabwe Coalition's office in South Africa issued the press statement I had drafted:

> During the 16 Days of Activism, Zimbabwean women activists have been hard hit by the government's ongoing campaign against human rights defenders and activists. One of Zimbabwe's foremost human rights activists was abducted today by armed state agents and 10 women trade unionists were badly assaulted during a protest.

> Jestina Mukoko, the Director of the Zimbabwe Peace Project, a primary documentation institution, was abducted from her home in Norton, about 31 km from Harare, today, Wednesday 3 December, around 05h00 by armed plain clothed security

agents believed to be the Central Intelligence Organisation (CIO). The men were driving a Mazda Familia car without registration plates. They gained access to her home after assaulting her caretaker/guard. Her 17 year old son and her domestic worker witnessed the abduction. Ms Mukoko was taken away still wearing her nightdress.

Jestina Mukoko's organisation, Zimbabwe Peace Project, has produced meticulously-researched reports on partisan distribution of humanitarian and food assistance by the Zimbabwe government and the violence inflicted on Zimbabweans at community level. In past years Ms Mukoko was a news anchor for the state-owned Zimbabwe Broadcasting Corporation.

Another 10 women were heavily assaulted by the police in Harare, during a protest organised by the Zimbabwe Congress of Trade Unions (ZCTU). Those assaulted include Getrude Hambira (General Agricultural and Plantation Workers' Union – General Secretary), Angeline Chitambo (Zimbabwe Energy Workers' Union – President), Tecla Masamba (Communications and Allied Workers' Union of Zimbabwe), Martha Kajama (National Engineering Workers' Union of Zimbabwe) and Mirriam Katumba (Vice Chair Women's Advisory Council).

In Pretoria, a group of young refugee women, survivors of state-sponsored violence and abuse in Zimbabwe, have been holding a picket in Church Street, in front of Union Buildings, in protest against the ongoing violence and abuse of women by Zimbabwean government State agents. They are vehemently opposed to continued Zanu PF control of Zimbabwe's security ministries.

Numerous organisations issued press statements on that fateful day. The Zimbabwe Human Rights Forum, of which Jestina was a board member, expressed deep concern, particularly in the light of a series of similar abductions in preceding months. Women of Zimbabwe Arise laid the blame squarely at the door of state agents and called on all solidarity networks to call Norton police station, the one closest to Jestina's home, to demand her immediate release: 'To state agents who took her our message is simple: your identity will not remain a secret and you will be held accountable – we are mobilising – the world is watching.'

In South Africa, a group of organisations – the Centre for the Study of Violence and Reconciliation, the Institute for Justice and Reconciliation, the Institute for Democracy in Southern Africa, Freedom House Southern Africa and the Heinrich Boll Foundation Southern Africa – organised an emergency meeting and issued a joint statement calling on the South African government and other regional leaders to act decisively by demanding the immediate release of Jestina Mukoko; to put further pressure on the Zimbabwean government to abandon the use of terror and intimidation and to use every type of leverage at their disposal for the quick resolution of Zimbabwe's crisis. It noted that, according to the Global Political Agreement (GPA) signed by Zimbabwe's main political parties on 15 September 2008, the Zanu-PF regime had a responsibility to ensure that all state security structures respected the rule of law, that militia groups were disbanded and that those responsible for abuses were held to account.

I returned home, exhausted, to find another sad message, one that seemed to be a fitting bookmark to the end of a tragic day. The poetic tribute to a fallen comrade by the young activist Sam Farai Monro, known as Comrade Fato, captured the misery of the moment.

Die For the People

Today we paused for a moment of silence. Silence amidst the echoes of cholera cries, mutinous outbursts and beaten trade unionists. We paused for a moment, calm in the chaos of our struggle. We stood by a red dust Warren Hill graveside to remember our Comrade Fela. A comrade who tirelessly fought in the trade unions, the Zimbabwe Social Forum and the residents associations. A founding member of the Uhuru Network and The Amandla Centre.

A comrade who died from the injustice he fought so hard against.

A collapsed health care system that failed to give him basic treatment.

We stood. We cried. We paused for a moment of reflection in the whirlwind that this struggle for justice can be. Because this is what it can be sometimes. Life or death painted in stark red soil. Each shovel-load of soil by each comrade onto his coffin was a reminder of the urgency of the struggle we are in. Each speech about Fela's life was a call to uprising.

Fela died as he lived. Determined. Dignified. His death was poetic. Because he fulfilled the destiny of his name. Die For The People.

May our comrade rest in peace.

Profoundly moved by these words, I wondered how long it would be before we would have to be crafting similar messages in memory of Jestina. Would a year that had been marked by such sadness and suffering end with yet another tragedy?

The year 2008 was truly an *annus horribilis* (horrible year) for the people of Zimbabwe. The education system collapsed under the weight of the economic crisis and the security situation resulted in the closure of many schools and tertiary institutions for most of the year. Neglect of infrastructure and mismanagement of water systems had led to a cholera epidemic that killed thousands and spread beyond Zimbabwe's borders, placing an intolerable burden on health systems in neighbouring countries. A collapse in veterinary services led to outbreaks of anthrax and foot and mouth disease, a devastating blow to the beef industry, a mainstay of Zimbabwe's beleaguered economy.

Warnings that Zimbabwe was fast becoming a regional catastrophe had become a reality. Zimbabwean opposition politician David Coltart's summary of the situation was apposite. He described Zimbabwe as being in the vortex of a perfect humanitarian storm: 'an unprecedented convergence of AIDS, poverty, hyperinflation, malnutrition, a regime that does not care and now, cholera'.

To understand this 'perfect storm' one needs to go back to 2000, when four dramatic developments transformed Zimbabwe's political and economic landscape. The first was the inaugural congress of a new political party, the Movement for Democratic Change, on 26 January 2000 and the election of former ZCTU leader Morgan Tsvangirai as its president. The second was the rejection of the government's proposed constitution in the referendum of February 2000. This was the first defeat of the ruling party by any national vote since independence in 1980 and it marked a new era of confrontation between government and the growing opposition movement.

Shaken by the rejection of the proposed constitution, the Zanu-PF government responded in the same month with a series of orchestrated invasions of white-owned farmland, an operation euphemistically referred to as 'fast-track land reform'. This chaotically administered land reform resulted in an economic crisis of staggering proportions, characterised by de-industrialisation, mass unemployment and rampant inflation that squeezed the livelihoods of the working class and led to a collapse in social, health and education services.

The catastrophic decrease in food production caused a humanitarian crisis that reduced large sections of Zimbabwe's population to complete dependence on Western food aid. The food security of the rural population was further compromised by the politicisation of food aid, especially around election time, by the denial of aid to those perceived to be opposition supporters.

The fourth dramatic development was the emergence of the newly-formed MDC as a major political force when it won 46.5% of the vote in the June parliamentary election. The Zanu-PF government responded by sharpening its armoury of repressive measures and deploying them during subsequent elections. From 2000 onwards Zimbabweans endured nine by-elections and parliamentary or presidential elections in 2002, 2005 and 2008, all of them marked by widespread intimidation through systematic state-sponsored violence and disenfranchisement by various means such as confiscation of identity documents, manipulation of the voters' roll and a sustained and ongoing propaganda campaign that legitimised violence against all opposition forces on the grounds that they were agents of the West. These elections served to deepen Zimbabwe's multi-faceted crisis.

A major consequence of the political turmoil and economic collapse was the massive exodus of Zimbabweans from their country of birth. It is estimated that more than four million have left the country since 2000, mainly to South Africa, the United Kingdom, Australia, Canada and other countries in the Southern African Development Community (SADC) region. The emigration of health workers, teachers, journalists and engineers and other professionals has contributed to a disastrous brain drain.

Regional efforts to resolve Zimbabwe's political crisis were spearheaded by the then South African president, Thabo Mbeki, who tried, as early as 2003, to get Zanu-PF and the MDC to negotiate a political settlement. Mbeki's position as the chief mediator of the Zimbabwean conflict was formally confirmed at an emergency SADC summit convened in response to the brutal beatings and arrest on 11 March 2007 of prominent MDC and civil society leaders, including MDC president Morgan Tsvangirai. Even President Robert Mugabe's allies could not ignore the shocking images of the battered and bruised leaders and SADC exerted strong pressure on both Mugabe and Tsvangirai to arrive at an agreement on a process leading to elections whose result would be acceptable to all parties.

Far from being credible and acceptable, the Zimbabwean electoral process that began relatively peacefully in March 2008 descended into one of the most bizarre and bloody in recent times. Counting at the polling booths revealed that the electorate had handed the MDC a resounding victory in the combined presidential, parliamentary, senate and local government elections held on 29 March. The government responded by withholding the presidential election results for one month, then claiming that the result was indecisive and necessitated a run-off between Mugabe and Tsvangirai.

The veneer of democracy painted over the 29 March poll was stripped away and, throughout April and May 2008, the people of Zimbabwe faced the full brunt of state-sponsored brutality that was unprecedented even by Zimbabwe's bloody standards. The deployment of SADC observers in mid-June failed to stem the violence. Prevented from campaigning, with more than 200 members confirmed dead, more than 2 000 severely assaulted, hundreds of women raped and sexually abused and thousands displaced, the MDC was forced to withdraw one week before the 27 June poll.

Against the advice of the United Nations, the African Union and SADC, the Zimbabwean government proceeded with the 27 June run-off election and, in the face of world condemnation, Robert Mugabe was declared victorious and inaugurated as president of Zimbabwe one day after the election, in time for him to attend the 11th African Union Ordinary Summit in Sharm El Sheikh in Egypt on 1 July 2008.

The sham election of 27 June was, correctly, given the thumbs down by the Pan-African Parliament, the AU and the SADC observer missions. Despite expressing concern about the negative reports of the observer missions, the violence and loss of life in Zimbabwe and the need to avert an escalation of conflict, the AU at the Sharm El Sheikh summit did not recommend any substantive action against the Mugabe regime. It merely threw the fate of the Zimbabwean people back into the hands of the SADC-appointed mediator, President Mbeki, urging him to continue to seek a negotiated solution in the form of a government of national unity. So, after risking their lives to vote for the government of their choice, the majority of Zimbabweans were back where they started.

As if that was not enough, in May 2008 simmering xenophobic resentment of African 'foreigners' exploded into large-scale attacks on migrant African communities throughout South Africa, resulting in the deaths of more than 60 people. By virtue of their numbers, Zimbabweans were the most affected. Several Zimbabweans were killed and thousands of others suffered assaults, loss of property and severe emotional and psychological trauma.

The Mbeki-led mediation process proceeded against a background of continued violence, insecurity and increasing starvation, exacerbated by the Zimbabwe government's ban on humanitarian aid on 3 June 2008. President Mbeki succeeded in getting Mugabe, Tsvangirai and Arthur Mutambara of the smaller MDC faction to sign a Global Political Agreement on 15 September 2008 at Rainbow Towers in Harare. Hopes that the deal would bring some relief to the beleaguered population were quickly dashed by intractable disputes that the SADC summit of 27 October 2008 and subsequent mediation efforts failed to resolve.

The SADC political process did little to address the massive human rights violations and it was clear that the atrocities committed during the election period would simply be swept under the SADC carpet. Even as Robert Mugabe was signing the GPA, his security establishment was orchestrating a sinister campaign of enforced disappearances. Thirty individuals, including a two-year-old boy, were abducted between October 2008 and 3 December, the day Jestina disappeared.

At the time, I was deputy chairperson of the board of the Open Society Initiative of South Africa (OSISA). The ongoing human rights violations in Zimbabwe, especially Jestina's disappearance, dominated our board meeting discussion. Eddie Makue, the then general secretary of the South African Council of Churches (SACC), responded to our request to make a joint appeal. OSISA programme officer Isabella (Bella) Matambanadzo and I drafted a press statement that was released on Friday 5 December. The statement noted that it was more than 48 hours since Jestina's disappearance. The SACC and OSISA expressed grave concern that a woman had been forcibly taken from her home in front of her teenage son at a time when the region and the world as a whole was commemorating the 16 Days of Activism Against Violence Against Women

The statement named the thirty individuals who had been abducted since the signing of the GPA and stated:

> The abductions have targeted talented, gifted and courageous leaders in Zimbabwean communities across the country, like Mukoko.

> We echo the sentiments expressed by Zimbabwean civil society that this abduction is a mockery of the Global Political Agreement (GPA) signed by the major political parties on September 15, 2008. It shows the extent of the breakdown of the Rule of Law and bad faith of the state authorities in Zimbabwe.

> It further confirms the concerns of the people of Zimbabwe about the ability of the security forces to act in the public interest in an impartial and professional manner.

The SACC and OSISA demanded that the security establishment in Zimbabwe and the guarantors of the September 15 Global Political Agreement – SADC and the African Union – ensure the immediate and unconditional release of Jestina Mukoko and all other individuals being illegally held by the state authorities in Zimbabwe and the immediate end to state purges, violence and organised torture by security agents.

Not only did the Zimbabwean security agents ignore local, regional and international appeals to release Jestina, they continued their sinister campaign with breathtaking impunity. The following week saw the enforced disappearances of Zacharia Nkomo, brother of Harrison Nkomo, one of the lawyers working on Jestina's case, and two of Jestina's colleagues, Broderick Takawira and Pascal Gonzo, journalist Shadreck Manyere and MDC officials Gandhi Mudzingwa and Chris Dlamini.

Our fears for Jestina's life increased. Zimbabwean police confirmed in writing that they did not have her in their custody and a judge could not be found to hear the habeas corpus application submitted by her lawyers. The Crisis Coalition's South Africa office, a network of South African civil society organisations that made up the Zimbabwe Solidarity Forum (ZSF) put together a 'Justice for Jestina' campaign against enforced disappearances in Zimbabwe, its key message being: 'an injury to one is an injury to all – don't allow enforced disappearances in your neighbourhood'.

The campaign helped to assist Zimbabwean activists who had been forced to seek temporary refuge in South Africa to escape the threat of abduction. The publicity aspect of the campaign targeted key decision-makers in South Africa and the public in general about the abductions. Zimbabwe Solidarity Forum leaders Sipho Theys and Richard Smith worked closely with Nina Tawanda of Norwegian People's Aid to find a way to secure emergency funding during a time when bureaucracies were closed for the holidays.

Bella Matambanadzo, the late Charlotte Schaer and I worked like women possessed to put together a proposal and to organise campaign materials. Because it was the December holiday period our offices were closed and I recall afternoons of intense discussions and strategising in Charlotte's kitchen garden in Observatory. We had to find the resources to host some of the Zimbabwe Peace Project staff who feared for their safety because, following the abductions of their colleagues, they noted that they were under surveillance by strange and unknown persons.

Among the many media interviews we gave at the time, one stands out in my mind. Bella, Nixon and I were interviewed by Udi ya-Nakamhela on SABC Africa. Throughout the interview the young Namibian journalist issued appeals to the public for any information about Jestina and gave a number to call. As we left the studio he told us that the appeals would not stop until Jestina was found. 'How can we, as Africans, allow something like this? She could be my mother!' he said, his voice shaking with emotion.

A couple of days later he contacted us to say he had received threatening text messages, one of them directed at Bella: 'Beware mwana wamatam-banadzo be abducted very soon (sic) I fear 4 u.' Bella continued to work undeterred, but the message served as a sober reminder of the sinister nature of the forces we were confronting.

The misery, despair and horror of that period was allayed somewhat by the unprecedented level of solidarity from organisations and individuals across the political spectrum and racial and religious divides. Jestina's abduction struck a chord. It seemed to be the straw that broke the camel's back of the Mugabe regime's abuses.

The support from women's organisations and African feminist networks was extraordinary. I will never forget the passionate statement made by activist Siphomthati Mthati about the war against the people of Zimbabwe. 'It has a name! It has a face! It is being fought across the bodies of women, men and children who are like prisoners in their own country ...'

South African activists like Sipho, Bunie Sexwale, Charlotte Schaer, Bibi Khan and many others were unstinting in their support. Elizabeth Mokotong mobilised women in church networks and put us in touch with a group of ANC women who assured us: 'We are not going to let this matter rest. We are taking it up to the highest offices.' Senior ANC official Jessie Duarte ensured a statement from the ANC secretary-general, expressing concern about the situation.

Our campaign took us to Botswana, where some of the threatened activists had fled. We were hosted there by Alice Mogwe and her team at Ditshwanelo, the Botswana Centre for Human Rights. It is difficult to describe the support and inspiration they provided. I had not experienced such a level of solidarity since I had started working for the regional advocacy programme for the Crisis in Zimbabwe Coalition at the end of 2003.

One of the most distressing aspects of that work was to be confronted constantly by an anti-imperialist discourse that held up Robert Mugabe and Zanu-PF as the vanguard of a glorious revolution and described all criticism of Mugabe as Western-sponsored and inspired. This Manichean view of Zimbabwean politics informed the policies of most SADC leaders, especially the mediator, President Thabo Mbeki. It is a view that led directly to the suppression of criticism and often to the outright denial of the extent of human rights violations in Zimbabwe. However, even the most ardent supporters of Robert Mugabe and his regime found it difficult to defend the orchestrated state-sponsored violence of the June presidential run-off election and the abductions that followed.

On 19 December Morgan Tsvangirai issued the threat that we believed was long overdue. He warned that if the abductions did not stop immediately and all abductees were not released or charged by 1 January 2009 he would ask the MDC's national council to pass a resolution to suspend all negotiations and contact with Zanu-PF. 'There can be no meaningful talks while a campaign of terror is being waged against our people,' he said.

On 23 December the news came that 32 of the 'disappeared' activists, including Jestina Mukoko, had been located in prisons around Harare. It was the best Christmas gift we could have received.

The appearance of Jestina and the others in court on 24 December was, in part, due to the persistence of the families, lawyers and organisations of the abductees. The diplomatic community in Harare, which held Jestina in high regard, played its part, as did pressure from international governments and appeals from prominent figures such as the UN secretary-general and the UN High Commissioner for Human Rights. I would also like to think our regional solidarity campaign had some impact.

However, I believe the factor that weighed heaviest was the prospect of the MDC pulling out of the Global Political Agreement that was to lead to the Government of National Unity (GNU) in 2009. Mugabe and his lieutenants needed the lifeline the GNU provided and however much they held the MDC in contempt, they needed their cooperation.

The ordeal of the abductees was far from over and they still had to suffer through one of the most farcical trials in Zimbabwe's legal history. I will not go into that because Jestina provides an account of it in her compelling memoir, but I cannot resist sharing my reflections about one of the hearings I attended.

I had been struck by the dilapidated state of the once-elegant building; the parquet floors were now dull and dusty and the stink of the toilets followed one through the corridors, right into the courtroom. Sadly, the kind of justice dispensed in the courtroom stank even more than the toilets. To label the performance of the state prosecutor, Florence Ziyambe, as incompetent would be to do her a kindness.

In what should be recorded as one of the most mind-boggling and inept performances witnessed in a court of law, Ms Ziyambe argued that the Attorney-General's office was not able to serve the indictment because the documents could not be prepared because 'the machine was broken'. She did not specify which machine. The coffee machine? The printer? The photocopy machine? Alex Muchadehama, the defence lawyer, stood head and shoulders above the magistrate and prosecutor (literally and figuratively) when he argued that his clients should not be made to suffer further because of the incompetence of the AG's office.

Jestina Mukoko's ordeal affected me profoundly. Her account of detention, torture, trial on trumped up charges, being forced to report to the police, every week, not being able to move freely, reminds me of the experiences of my own mother-in-law, Albertina Sisulu.

Indeed, Jestina's quiet reserve and dignified demeanour reminds me very much of the gravitas of MaSisulu. Like MaSisulu, Jestina has been a consistent, hardworking leader, utterly dependable, a rock within her family and within the peace-building and human rights community. MaSisulu said time and again that she had fought her struggles for future generations. It pains me deeply that Jestina was denied the freedoms that women like MaSisulu fought for, in what is supposed to be a free country.

It pains me that Zimbabwe's Government of National Unity failed to address the unfinished business of human rights abuses. Reading through the accounts of the abductees, I am struck by the suffering they continued to endure in the aftermath of their ordeals. They have received no acknowledgement from the state of the harm that was done to them, no apology and no redress.

Those responsible for the enforced disappearances and the horrific acts perpetrated on the disappeared have never been held to account. Because they have gotten away scot-free, the threat of enforced disappearances remains a reality in Zimbabwe. Jestina Mukoko has spoken out against the abduction of activist Itai Dzamara in broad daylight on 9 March 2015 by men who identified themselves as police. Itai has not been seen since.

Reading this memoir was a deeply emotional experience for me and on several occasions I could barely continue. The story is powerful and poignant and I can imagine what it cost Jestina to revisit the most traumatic period of her life. Not only is her story a powerful personal narrative, it is also a very important piece of social and political history. As accounts of confinement and interrogation go, it is right up there with classic works such as Ruth First's *117 Days* and *The Jail Diary of Albie Sachs*.

It is my hope that Jestina's memoir will sensitise citizens of this region to the dangers of enforced disappearances and encourage all of us to adopt the approach that an injury to one is an injury to all. Historical examples from Latin America demonstrate the havoc that this practice can wreak on a society. The threat of one enforced disappearance is a threat to all of us.

Elinor Sisulu
Johannesburg
April 2016

| Political Background

Zimbabwe (formerly Rhodesia) gained its independence from British colonial rule in 1980. After that date it was governed first by the Zimbabwe African National Union (Zanu) and, since 1987, when Zanu and the Patriotic Front Zimbabwe African People's Union (Zapu) merged, by the Zimbabwe African National Union Patriotic Front (Zanu-PF); always under the leadership of Robert Mugabe.

In 2008, however, the party faced its first real challenge from the Movement for Democratic Change (MDC), headed by former union leader Morgan Tsvangirai. The MDC was later to split into factions, the largest, led by Tsvangirai, known as MDC-T.

In that year the country held two elections. The March harmonised poll (to elect both president and parliament) concluded with no outright winner as Tsvangirai fell short of the required 50% votes plus one to take the presidency. As stipulated in the country's constitution, a presidential run-off was scheduled for 27 June 2008 but Tsvangirai withdrew, citing increasing violence against his supporters, more than 200 of whom had lost their lives in escalating violence.

Tsvangirai and Mugabe, urged by the Southern African Development Community (SADC) and the African Union (AU) to negotiate a political settlement, signed a Global Political Agreement (GPA) on 15 September. The agreement was facilitated by then South African president, Thabo Mbeki. The GPA was expected to pave the way for the implementation of much needed reforms of institutions and laws that would lead to free and fair elections in the future.

Prologue

I trudge into courtroom 6. It is 15 January 2009 and this is my fourth court appearance since Christmas Eve 2008. The trial was supposed to start at 11h15 but the prosecution team was more than an hour late. My three brothers, with their trademark bald heads, and my son, Takudzwa, lined up in the first row, are all wearing sullen faces. I avoid looking my son in the eye; somehow I feel I have failed him as a mother.

I, one of five fellow female prisoners, am conscious that my discomfort, exacerbated by steel clanking against the wooden floors with every step I take, is observed by many in the courtroom.

My elder brother, Cosmas, stops reading the newspaper in his hand and gazes at me as I squeeze myself into a space on the bench in the dock. As I scan the courtroom, which is bursting at its seams, I notice a number of my relatives and acknowledge their presence with a nod, since my hands are confined. A significant number of civil society colleagues are craning their necks from the doorway to catch a glimpse of me. Some send eye signals, others simply shake their heads in disbelief.

There is a dispute between the two teams of lawyers – the defence team seems to be protesting about something. Initially they speak in low voices. Alec Muchadehama, part of my defence team approaches the dock, then shakes his head in disapproval as he walks towards the rest of the defence team. He whispers something to my feisty lawyer, Swaziland-born Beatrice Mtetwa, one of Zimbabwe's renowned human rights lawyers, who has been asked by Zimbabwe Lawyers for Human Rights to lead the defence team.

2

Alec confirms that all of us are in handcuffs and leg irons, apart from Violet Mupfuranhewe, who has her two-year-old son, Nigel, with her. The team of prosecutors seems unmoved by these protestations.

As soon as the magistrate, Archie Wochiunga, is in his seat, the defence team calls his attention to the problem and the magistrate immediately orders the prison officers to unshackle me and my fellow prisoners as well as four male prisoners who are standing as there is no space for them to sit. When this is done I see a slight sign of relief on the faces in the courtroom. Beatrice asks to consult with me. 'Are you still up to taking to the witness stand to give your own account?' she asks. I feel strong and willing to tell the court and my family what happened from the moment I disappeared and inform her of this.

Before I take the witness stand, Beatrice tells the court that my rights have been violated in many ways. She says when I was snatched from home I was not told why I was being taken away, I have not had access to my lawyers and my family and neither the Attorney General nor the police provided the protection of the law. She goes on to argue that this deprivation of my liberty, let alone the inhuman and degrading punishment, is not constitutional.

'If it pleases this court I wish to call the applicant to the witness stand,' announces Beatrice. The prison officer watching over us opens the dock and I see everyone in the courtroom trying to stand up to see my entire frame as I walk towards the witness stand. In five weeks this is the closest I have come to tasting freedom.

I'm dressed in a bright green pleated chemise dress, white trainers and thick white socks on a hot summer day. The thick socks cushion the legs to ease the pain caused by the leg irons, ordinarily reserved for prisoners who are high escape risks, or those who have committed very serious offences. I've lost a great deal of weight in the few weeks that I have been detained incommunicado.

After the court formalities of swearing on the Bible that I will tell the truth, the whole truth and nothing but the truth, Beatrice, addresses me. 'Jestina, kindly give this honourable court details of what happened in the 21 days that we knew nothing about your whereabouts.' This is the first time even my family will hear me speak about what happened in

3

the days of darkness when they were uncertain whether they would ever see me alive again.

Narrating the experience to the packed courtroom I relive the interrogation, the torture, the death threats and the breakdown. The magistrate adjourns the hearing to the afternoon. As the prison officers lead me from the witness stand I notice my son leaving the courtroom in a hurry as though he wants to escape and my three brothers wiping away tears and avoiding looking at me.

My lawyers have made a court application challenging my prosecution. The law, they assert, has failed to protect me and they want my case to be referred to the Supreme Court, sitting as the Constitutional Court. I pray that they will succeed.

It is well after lunchtime when the court officials take a break. As soon as we leave the courtroom we are handcuffed and the leg irons are restored. We are led downstairs to the underground cells. There are stagnant pools of sewage water all over the place and raw sewage in some places. It is quite a feat to avoid the pools of foul-smelling water in leg irons with hands confined. The route to the underground cells is like a dungeon, there are no lights and the leg irons make it very difficult to walk down a circular staircase in the dark. The nine of us held hands and walked like ants, in single file, until we reached the foot of the staircase, where there is some light.

The prison officers find something to talk about and keep their spirits high as they walk behind us. They imitate Beatrice, 'She was kept incommunicado,' begins one. 'Since I started working and have been accompanying inmates to court I have never heard "incommunicado",' retorts another. All the inmates are in stitches when one of the officers announces, 'I need to get lunch before I find myself incommunicado.' So, for the rest of the day and on the trip back to the prison there is talk of 'incommunicado'.

A terrible stench in the cell forces us to huddle together close to the bars of the door for fresh air. This does not go down well with the prison officers, who seem determined that we should endure the stench. One of them, Jane, comes close to exchanging blows with us after uttering some harsh words.

'Some of you think because you are human rights people you see yourself as special. Well, here we do not have special people and I can

4

beat the hell out of all of you. Move back before I reorganise you,' she warns, charging towards the cell, keys in hand, ready to deal with us. Harrison Nkomo, who was working with Beatrice Mtetwa, arrives just in time, bringing food. 'What is the problem? Officer please let us not get to that, allow me to talk to them,' Harrison pleads with Jane, who stops before she reaches the bars of the cell.

On this day two of the important women in my life, *mbuya* Mukoko, my mother and my mother-in-law, *gogo* Dizha, are not in court. I learned later that my brothers, son and nephew have left them at home, worried that they would become too emotional and that *mbuya* Mukoko complained to Dr Sanyanga - whose father is my maternal grandmother's nephew - that 'they think I don't understand the language in court, but just being in the court and seeing her in the dock pacifies me'. The boys tell me that she detests the name 'Florence', the name of the prosecutor.

In the courtroom the silence and concentration is frightening as everyone, including the journalists and international diplomats who fill some of the seats, listen to what happened to me at the hands of state security agents since 3 December.

When I speak about the beatings on the soles of my feet, there are moments of silence as I try to fight back tears. 'Do you think you can continue?', the magistrate wants to know, and I respond in the affirmative.

'Your Worship, I pray that this court realises that this application is vexatious and frivolous. The applicant has other avenues of remedy; she can be compensated.' The prosecutor, Florence Ziyambi, makes this statement with her eyes on me as if to bait me with the useless Zimbabwe dollars that are legal tender at this time. Inflation in Zimbabwe is the highest in the world at the time and most Zimbabweans are trillionaires.

Court is adjourned to the next day at 15h00 for a ruling. At the end of the proceedings I dread the formalities of being handcuffed and put in leg irons but that is the order of the day when you are a class D prisoner. In the underground cells we are ready to take our ride in the red van back to Chikurubi Maximum Security Prison. Two, at times, three vehicles from the Support Unit escort the red van to and from the prison.

Seventy-two-year-old *sekuru* (grandfather) Fidelis Chiramba, one of the MDC-T activists who were abducted from Banket, has passengers in stitches as he details his torture, 'As old as I am I had no idea that extreme cold can be hot. I was once locked in a deep freezer only to be released and dipped in hot water. The cruel people once paraded me naked in front of these young women here and when they looked down they were ordered to take note of my body geography.' The women he is referring to are Violet Mupfuranhewe and Pieta Kaseke, another female MDC-T activist from Banket, who were sharing a room with him.

A former police officer, *sekuru* Chiramba says his family always knew he was alive. He sends text messages from the phone of one of the operatives, who, I learnt during my time in custody, has the same name as my brother Cosmas, although it is not clear if it is his real name. While *sekuru* Chiramba was in custody the police at one time tried to mislead his sons and deny that he was there. The boys remembered what their father had taught them about police handover sessions; at handover those knocking off are obliged to shout the names of inmates and give details related to why they are in custody. They went to a police station where the police denied knowledge of the detention of their father and listened during the handover only to hear *sekuru* Fidelis Chiramba's name being called out.

My Story

I was born in 1967 at a modest clinic in Mutapa, an old suburb of Gweru a few months before my paternal grandmother was called to glory. I inherited both my grandmother's names, Jestina Mungarewa, and automatically became my father's mother. My grandmother was overjoyed that her name would continue to be used after she died. She had hoped that my elder sister would carry her name but this was not to be.

My aunt, my father's only biological sibling, died a few months after giving birth to her only daughter, Margaret. When my mother was in labour with my sister she had to travel to Bulawayo, where there were specialists to attend to her. There she was hosted by my late aunt's husband and daughter in one of the low-density suburbs (reserved for whites), where my aunt's husband worked as a domestic helper and it was they who took the liberty of naming my sister Jennifer after my late aunt.

6

As a child I was inquisitive about the meaning of my names. My mother did not know the meaning of Jestina, but Mungarewa, according to my grandmother, means, 'people can say whatever they want as it does not change anything'.

My mother, Laina, a devout Anglican, was widowed in 1972 when I was five and my youngest sibling, Simon, was two. My father, Agrippa, a glazier and house painter, fell to his death from the ladder on which he was working. My mother lives in Mambo, one of the old high-density suburbs (where the black majority live) in Gweru, a city some 279km south of Harare. I am the younger of two girls in a family of eight, one of whom is a half-brother, my father's son.

For as long as I can remember my mother has grown vegetables and other crops. In doing so, she was able to provide for the family – we never needed to buy mealies and we always had our maize meal ground rather than having to buy commercial meal. We also enjoyed other delicacies, like pumpkins, traditional cucumbers and sweet potatoes.

My mother was an enterprising woman, who, during her younger years, made and sold doilies to raise money for the upkeep of the family after my father died. Every month my mother would travel to tourist resorts to sell her wares – either in the resort town of Victoria Falls or in Bulawayo. In all the years that she travelled to Victoria Falls, though, she had neither the time nor the interest to visit the Falls I was able to take her there when she was 83 and she was amazed at the 'smoke that thunders'.

We always knew the month had been good if, when she returned, she pounded rice from her field, mashed it with peanut butter and plucked a chicken for a special meal. As long as I can remember, however, when we did have chicken we would also always have visitors and the meat intended for the children would be reduced or a different relish would be provided as the visitors were fed.

When we were children it was common practice to sit around a plate of sadza (a thick porridge made from ground maize) or rice with peanut butter and relish, which could either be vegetables in a peanut butter sauce or meat. When we had meat for a meal a protocol had to be followed.

7

The eldest had the first serving of meat and the youngest would wait until everyone had their share. It was a serious offence, punishable with a good hiding, if the youngest had meat before the eldest. If the eldest wanted to punish the younger ones, he or she would continue to eat the sadza and the sauce without touching the meat. Every time this happened I told myself that when I grew up, I would have my revenge.

My mother was a disciplinarian. I think having been widowed and left with six young children she needed to assert her authority. But she did not believe in meting out justice during the day. She would have her whip ready under her bed and after the evening meal, if any one deserved to be disciplined, she would say, 'Follow me to the bedroom I want to send you somewhere before it gets dark.' If the key turned after her you knew you would be getting your punishment. When the grandchildren came, however, this aspect of her character simply faded.

In her old age, with no children in her house, she stopped selling doilies but refused to give up looking after her vegetable garden as well as the other crops she cultivated in larger fields demarcated by the local authority. Whenever we visit she packs fresh as well as dried products from the fields. My eldest brother, John, lives on a farm close to Gweru. Cosmas and Peter also live in Gweru, while Simon at the tme lived a few houses away from me on the same street in Norton, a small town west of Harare.

Four of my siblings have passed away. Canaan, three years older than me and also known as 'KC', passed away in October 2000. He had been in and out of hospital for several months before that. He was an intriguing character. Generally happy, he would at times unexpectedly retreat into his shell.

My only sister, Jennifer, a humble, no-nonsense, hard-working person, died suddenly and unexpectedly three years after Canaan, while visiting me in Harare before I moved to Norton. She had been unwell for just a day and died after being admitted to hospital. Our sisters-in-law had dubbed her 'manager' because of her ability to stand up to her brothers when they misbehaved.

Robson, my father's second son and my mother's first, passed away in 2004. A fountain that oozed love and selflessness, he sacrificed a great deal when my mother was widowed. Robson, unlike friends his age, got married late in life and assumed the role of father figure to the family. He collapsed while watering his garden after work and by the time the paramedics arrived he had taken his last breathe. Canaan remains etched in most of our minds as my mother, even 16 years after his passing, still calls his name several times every single day. It is common to hear her: '*Iwe* (You), Canaan' (when she calls the grand children) or '*Canaan, ndisvitse banga iro* (Canaan, hand me that knife)'.

Simon the youngest of the family and the one who filed court applications after the abduction succumbed to a stomache ailment in January 2010 on my mother's birthday. Of my siblings Simon is the one I fought with most because of his temperament. When he joined the church in Norton he became peace loving and calmer.

As a young girl I admired my teacher, Mrs Ndlovu, at Sandara primary school and my initial dreams were centred on becoming a teacher like Mrs Ndlovu, who lived in the same street as we did in Mambo. Every morning I would go past her house to pick up anything she wanted taken to school. She became my role model and I would see myself in a classroom and would imagine children passing through my home in their clean uniforms to pick up a variety of things to take to school. I became a teacher briefly and did not like it, but somehow I think what I have turned out to be is in line with my initial ambitions. As leader of a growing human rights organisation, the Zimbabwe Peace Project, I am constantly disseminating information in order to create awareness about the human rights situation as well as suggesting ways of ensuring that human rights are not only protected and respected, but also fulfilled.

When I was nine I went to live with my cousin Margaret in Magwegwe, Bulawayo, Zimbabwe's second city, where I entered grade three at Mhali Primary School. It was here that I, whose mother tongue is chiShona, learnt to speak isiNdebele.

Looking back, I recognise that political trouble always seems to have stalked me. When I was in Form 1 at Eveline Girls High School in Bulawayo there was an uprising by war veterans in Entumbane and our household was among those targeted because we were Shona speaking. For several days we were woken up by stones thrown on the roof of the house. This

9

lasted until the police, responding to a complaint we had lodged, waylaid the perpetrators and were able to apprehend them. We felt unsafe in the neighbourhood and later moved.

By the time I wrote my A' levels (Advanced level examinations) I was back in Gweru, at Fletcher High School, where I became head girl. I was then accepted at the University of Zimbabwe, where I graduated in 1989 with a Bachelor of Science Honours degree in Politics and Administration.

I taught for several months between 1990 and 1992, starting at St Patrick's Secondary School in Chiwundura communal lands near Gweru, then at Matinunura Secondary School in Mkoba 9 high-density suburb in Gweru. In 1990 I was traditionally married to Herbert Dizha and in 1991 our son, Takudzwa Takura, was born. He was only four years old when his father passed away, succumbing to a chest infection.

It was while I was at Matinunura that Herbert, who knew I was not born to be a teacher, spotted an advertisement for candidates fluent in both chiShona and isiNdebele, which were the main indigenous languages in Zimbabwe.

It was only later, during a series of interviews, that I found out that the advertisement had been placed by the Zimbabwe Broadcasting Corporation (ZBC). I was to spend more than ten years as a broadcast journalist with the ZBC, starting as a radio newsreader before becoming an anchor on the prime time television news bulletin.

While working at the ZBC I met President Robert Mugabe, who had come to the studios to address the nation. I was on the late evening shift and the make-up artists had already knocked off. My neighbour, who worked in the president's office, asked me to do his make-up, using my own supplies. When I got to the studio, make-up in hand, I was told to wait until I was officially introduced. 'This is Jestina Mukoko, she is going to do your make-up.' As I walked towards the president he smiled and said, 'you have to make me look good'.

After my stint at the ZBC I moved into public relations, working briefly at the Westgate Shopping Mall, but continued to present the news on a part-time basis. Concerned by deteriorating journalistic ethics, I left the ZBC for good, joining two fellow journalists to form Radio Voice of the

People as a producer/reporter, a move that was to change my life.

It was my work there that was responsible for my shift into the field of human rights work. In 2002 I joined the Zimbabwe Civic Education Trust (ZIMCET), an organisation established to foster a culture of tolerance.

On one of my assignments in Matebeleland I interviewed several women who had been widowed during the Midlands and Matebeleland massacres of the 1980s. One story that remained etched in my mind was that of a woman who had been forced to witness her husband being buried alive – she had heard the screams of her loved one fade until she could not hear them anymore.

As I shared a simple but hearty meal with this woman in her kitchen I realised that she represented many other women in Matebeleland. Although I had been young at the time, I retained a vivid recollection of neighbours in Gweru having been beaten up because it was believed that they were members of Joshua Nkomo's Patriotic Front Zimbabwe African People's Union. I recall my mother shouting from her bedroom, adjacent to their semi-detached house, begging the attackers to spare them.

In 2007 I moved from ZIMCET to head the Zimbabwe Peace Project (ZPP), a non-governmental organisation (NGO) whose mandate is to monitor and document the politically-motivated violations and abuses of human rights that had been a debilitating cancer in the country for a long time. As national director of ZPP my role entailed overseeing all the programmes that fulfilled the mandate of the organisation. As a former journalist I recognised that the ZPP received a vast amount of critical human rights-related information but we needed to find ways of disseminating it.

The ZPP was established in 2000 in response to the political violence that wrought havoc in the aftermath of the constitutional referendum in which citizens voted against the government-proposed constitution. This was the first time in two decades that citizens had rejected a proposal by the Zanu-PF government. The ZPP monitored violence in both urban and rural areas from November 2001. The first election in which the organisation monitored and documented electoral violence was the presidential election of 2002.

11

Abduction

It was early evening on 2 December 2008, my last day of work before my annual vacation started. I had just had dinner and was relaxing at home in Norton and watching my daily dose of the American television soapie, *The Young and the Restless*. The show was so addictive I couldn't bear to miss an episode.

My son Takudzwa, 17, a lower sixth student at Midlands Christian College in Gweru and home from school for the holidays, and my six-year-old nephew, Tofara, son of my late brother Robson, were in the lounge with me, but they were busy with other things. Takudzwa, who was usually starved of his mobile phone during the school term, was fiddling with the gadget, well aware that disturbing me or fidgeting while the soapie was on was inviting trouble.

The house phone in the entrance hall rang, startling and briefly distracting me. I prayed that it wasn't for me. It rang for a while and before I could ask one of the boys to attend to it my domestic helper, MaDube, picked it up. '*mbuya* Mukoko is on the phone and she wants to speak to you,' she announced. *Mbuya* Mukoko is my mother, who, since the grandchildren arrived, we have stopped calling mother and refer to as grandmother Mukoko. I stood up and crossed the lounge, hoping to deal with the call as quickly as possible so that I could continue watching *The Young and the Restless*.

'I am extremely worried because I have a strong feeling something terrible is about to happen in the family,' she told me. 'While working in one of my fields this afternoon I saw a *tsuku kuviri* (a two-headed snake), not once, but twice, and I have had a strange feeling since then,' she said, her voice breaking.

I tried to pacify her, saying that the fields are habitats for snakes, but she was adamant. 'No, not that type of snake. I have had this dreadful feeling the whole day and can't eat.' I tried for a few minutes to calm her and encourage her to pray about it. I was conscious that I was missing out on *The Young and the Restless*.

When Takudzwa barged into my bedroom in the early hours of the next morning to announce that there were visitors at the gate I was irritated. On the first day of my vacation I was hoping to sleep in and was certainly not interested in entertaining visitors at that time of the day.

Later that day I was to be director of ceremonies at the Annual Auxilia Chimusoro Awards, funded by the United States Embassy and aimed at highlighting the courage and determination of Auxilia Chimusoro, the first woman in Zimbabwe to go public about her HIV status, in curbing the spread of HIV infection. Meanwhile, I hoped for a few more winks of sleep.

Having failed to wake me up, Takudzwa left, but in no time he was back and, as I prepared to tell him not to disturb me, he blurted out, 'Mama, the visitors at the gate are police officers.'

I got up, reached for my old and much-loved baby blue silk dressing gown, which was hanging behind the door, and walked towards the kitchen, my son in tow. Barefoot and wearing a stocking on my head to maintain my weave hairstyle, I was still tying the belt of the dressing gown when I found myself confronted by six grim-faced men and one woman, who were charging towards me like a pride of lions that has spotted its prey.

The dark, heavily-built man who seemed to be in charge of the team barked at me, 'Are you Jestina Mukoko?' His voice reverberated in the small space of the passage that leads to the kitchen. Almost losing my step, I confirmed that I was. To my surprise, as soon as I did so, two men firmly grabbed my hands as though they had found a treasure they had spent a long time searching for. MaDube the house help and Golden the gardener and security guard, with keys in hand, and who were in the kitchen, were tight lipped as they tried to make sense of what was unfolding.

My wrists began to hurt. The man holding my right hand said, as if to reassure those around me, 'We are police officers and only want you to look at some documents in our car and assist us with some information.' He fumbled in his pocket with his free hand and held out what seemed to be a card, but I couldn't read it as it was flashed close to my eyes and I was not wearing my prescription glasses. Although the man to my right who seemed quite young compared to all the others spoke the most,

13

the dark, heavily built man, who seemed to be a man of little words, was clearly in charge.

I looked into his bloodshot eyes and asked for time to dress decently. 'We do not have the time,' he responded, signalling that I must move. By this time Tofara was also up and confused by the goings on, but I had no chance to talk to him or to Takudzwa and, anyway, I didn't have a clue about what was happening.

I was force-marched out of the house towards the gate, where a silver grey unmarked Madza Familia was parked. The young man holding my right hand continued to speak until we reached the gate. 'Open the boot and take out that file so that we can show her.' He repeated this statement several times and gestured with his free hand as I tried to quietly negotiate an easing of the grip, but the more I moved my hand, the more his grip dug in.

The back passenger door was quickly opened and in a flash they bundled me into the car, where I found myself perched between two men. The man to my right had not been in the house, the one to my left was the one who had mentioned the file in the boot. He was young, perhaps about 30, with a light complexion. 'Put your head down,' commanded the man who appeared to be leading the team, who was sitting in the driver's seat, a dreadlocked woman beside him. The other men were not with us, I assumed they were in another vehicle.

The man to my right indicated that I should put my head on his lap. I tried to protest at having my head on the lap of an unknown man and as I obeyed, reluctantly, I noticed a rifle on the floor of the vehicle. This was clearly no ordinary arrest but at that stage I was not sure, if I was in the hands of the Zanu-PF militia – the youth group of the Zanu-PF party, or agents from the Central Intelligence Organisation, as both institutions are known for these types of acts. In fact, only a thin line separates the two institutions.

I assumed that we were driving in the direction of Harare, 40 km away from my home. The car went at very high speed and the music was so loud it could have ruptured an eardrum. My fellow passengers hardly spoke for much of the journey, which I estimate took between 35 and 40 minutes.

The journey was the worst I had ever endured. Driving at top speed with strangers who could be anyone and could do anything to me was unsettling enough without the thought of the rifle on the floor. Indecently dressed as I was, still in my night clothes, I feared being raped. So many thoughts flooded my mind as the vehicle raced towards its destination. What had I done to deserve this and what would they do to me? I had heard of people disappearing, never to be seen again and had seen images of people who had been brutally tortured.

A few minutes before the car stopped those in front used eye contact to announce that we were nearly at our destination. 'What time do you think we will get to Mutare?' asked the woman.

'We will get there very soon, you know how this machine moves,' replied the driver. Mutare, a city to the east of Harare, is more than three hours' drive away. I believe the question was a tactic to confuse me. The man on whose lap my head rested covered my face with something woollen. I protested that I could not breathe. He eased the covering, leaving only my eyes covered.

When the vehicle stopped I was confused because of the loud music from the radio. There was even louder music outside the car. I was led into a tiny room and rudely instructed to sit down. With my eyes still covered I groped around, trying to establish where I was going to sit. I knelt and then sat on the floor. The man who had led me into the room removed the woollen cover and, in a split second, replaced it with another. In that moment I saw that I was in what appeared to be a pantry in a government house. The floor was red and the shelves empty apart from a few unconnected analogue phones.

I was so afraid that I was unable to sit properly. I was shaking like a reed and having difficulty breathing. Would this nightmare ever end? The man walked out of the room, the door was locked and, officially, I was in detention. But where?

CHAPTER
two | Missing Person

The year 2008 had been an election year and violence had marked the run-up to the presidential run-off, leaving several people dead and many injured and maimed. I was well aware that Zanu-PF opposed the work of organisations like the Zimbabwe Peace Project, whose mandate was to expose the violence, and I knew that, as head of the organisation, I was vulnerable. During the run-up to the election I had stayed with friends on several occasions, but after the Global Political Agreement was signed I felt slightly more secure and did not anticipate any harm befalling me.

During the dangerous period I had educated Takudzwa on the basic steps to take if anything happened to me and made him understand the importance of raising the alarm with my colleagues at work, some of whom he had met.

Now that the worst had happened, I was worried about whether he would remember the security tips I had taught him. I would find out later that I need not have worried.

As the silver grey Mazda Familia disappeared into the rising sun Takudzwa, confused, paced the yard then went back into the house as if to trace my last steps. He felt, he was to tell me later, as though he was in some sort of lurid dream. One moment he was desperately trying to wake up his mother to attend to the strange visitors, the next, she was was gone and he didn't know whether he would ever see her again.

'Initially I just wanted to scream and let out all my fear and pain but there and then something hit me that if I did not act fast and let people know, I might not see you again,' he told me.

He rushed to my bedroom to look for my mobile phone to call one of my colleagues at ZPP, Broderick Takawira, the provincial coordinator for Harare province, hoping he might be able to help.

After calling lawyers and board members Broderick went to the office where he teamed up with another ZPP staffer, Tsitsi Mutongi (who has since passed away), in an effort to use their contacts in the police to find out what might have happened to me. Little did Broderick know that he would find out in less than a week exactly what had happened to me, but not in the way he was hoping.

He and his colleagues arranged to meet at the office on the Monday to collect and distribute missing person leaflets in the city centre, but while he was at the office with driver Pascal Gonzo they, too, received 'strange visitors' and were abducted.

My brother Simon and his wife Sibongile, were the first to arrive at the house after Takudzwa raised the alarm. My brother Cosmas, who was at the time in Bulawayo, 400km south of Harare, received the message about my disappearance from his son Tanaka, who had been contacted by Takudzwa. Initially he decided not to break the news to our mother, but Tanaka thought that was unwise. Cosmas and another brother, Peter, left their homes and families in Gweru for weeks on end to be in Norton to support Takudzwa and to search for their sister who had disappeared.

News of my disappearance and that of other ZPP staffers five days later spread like a raging veldfire. At the Auxilia Chimusoro awards, at which I should have been director of ceremonies, US Ambassador James McGee made a passionate plea to my abductors. 'We have been frantically searching for Jestina... We ask the people who have perpetrated this and whoever abducted her, be it the government or the police, to release her immediately. We need her to be released now.'

Simeon Mawanza, a colleague from Amnesty International who visited me after I was eventually granted bail, told me that Takudzwa had acted like a hero, passing on the message of my disappearance before I even reached the detention centre, enabling him to draft a statement immediately, launching a campaign that was taken up by the United Nations.

Amnesty International, which played a significant role during Zimbabwe's war of liberation, speaking against violations of human rights, played another important role during my detention, soliciting solidarity messages from all over the world.

My abduction was reported at Norton police station, a stone's throw from my house. Police who visited the scene – distancing themselves from those who abducted me – were shocked that someone could have been kidnapped from a house with such security – a perimeter wall electric fence and a number of vicious dogs. They also questioned the fact that Golden had opened the gate for these strangers.

Later that evening, when Cosmas and Peter arrived, it would emerge that the abductors had been seen in the neighbourhood and had, in fact visited the house on the previous Saturday.

Tofara told my brothers that the men had spoken to Golden some days earlier when he was walking Tofara home from school. It also turned out that they had asked neighbours about the people at my house and that on one occasion they had pretended to have a puncture and had taken time to fix it, all the while keeping an eye on the house.

On the Saturday before my abduction, when I, together with Takudzwa Tofara and some friends, had spent the day in Murewa, northeast of Harare only returning in the late evening, the men had come to the house. Golden had not told me of their visit.

Family members speculate that his hands might have been greased - the

18

economic situation in the country was desperate for all citizens.

When I was granted bail Golden was unable to speak to me. I think he felt responsible for my abduction and was ashamed to face me. Instead he wrote me a letter in which he tried to explain the difficult position he had found himself in when the operatives swooped.

In Harare, police at headquarters offered to place a missing person advertisement in the daily newspapers and to confirm, in a letter written by Assistant Commissioner Takawira Nzombe, who was responsible for legal affairs, that 'a crime has been committed and the abductors if found would answer charges of kidnapping'. However, when my incommunicado detention finally ended on 22 December, the police did not arrest the people responsible nor did they bother to inform my lawyers or my family about the fact that I had now been handed over to the police.

Other visitors to the house after my disappearance included lawyers, who advised Simon to file papers pertaining to my disappearance. As the sun disappeared below the western horizon the many people who had, since morning, been making a beeline for the house, disappeared and Takudzwa panicked. 'I did not think I would be safe in the house at night and I did not think being with *sekuru* Simon would have been any different from being alone in the house. Everyone knew he was your brother,' he confided later. 'As I tried to make sense of my situation I paced the house and the yard endlessly hoping and praying that some-one somewhere would think about me.'

For my son the house had been transformed within hours from a place of comfort, love and sanctuary into a detested place, he was afraid to be there alone.

His feelings of aloneness ended when the sound of the intercom buzzer revealed the presence of *mbuya mai* Alan (Aunty Mother of Alan), who took Takudzwa to her house for the night. *Mbuya mai* Alan married into the Sanyanga family, who have played a significant role both in my life and in that of the rest of the Mukoko family. *Sekuru* Davies Sanyanga, who is mai Alan's-father-in-law, is my paternal grandmother's nephew. As a result of this relationship our fathers were close and *sekuru* Sanyanga told us that before my father died each promised to watch over the other's

19

family if anything bad should happen. It was his daughter, Dr Rudo Sanyanga, who took Takudzwa in when she returned from Chiredzi. She also worked closely with the family in the search for me and was a source of comfort and support when I was granted bail.

The news of my disappearance became the subject of conversation in many civil society organisations that rallied to form search parties immediately after the incident. No-one expected the ordeal to go on for weeks and when it did, some people began to fear being associated with the action.

A lawyer friend, Otto Saki, said during one of his visits to Chikurubi that it had surprised him that 'there are people out there, some of them female lawyers, with certificates that enable them to visit you but who have to ask others how you are doing. It is absurd that in public some people do not want to be seen associating with you.'

While some feared that my fate would rub off on them, I was amazed by the courage and forthrightness of others, some of whom I already knew, some I did not, who took bold decisions to visit when I was in Chikurubi and when I was in hospital.

Some friends confided that for fear of being abducted without undergarments they had begun sleeping in shorts, others crossed the border to Botswana or South Africa for fear of the same fate befalling them. The women's movement, led by the Women's Coalition of Zimbabwe, to whom I had presented a paper on 2 December, approached Ms Oppah Muchinguri, a respected leader of the Zanu-PF party, for help.

Ms Muchinguri said she was keen to assist, but asked to meet my mother. Arrangements were made for the meeting, at which Ms Muchinguri assured my mother that she would help solve the mystery of my whereabouts.

Once I was out of prison and able to speak to my mother she praised Ms Muchinguri, who had phoned regularly to assure her that she was trying her best to get to the bottom of the matter. My lawyer, Beatrice, was convinced that if Ms Muchinguri had not been a member of Zanu-PF she would have taken to the streets to protest my disappearance.

When I did finally meet Ms Muchinguri she hugged me like a long-lost daughter. Three years later she told me she had not known what work I was doing and had put her head on a block, despite the fact that it made her unpopular, simply because I was a woman in trouble. A fighter in the liberation struggle that ushered in Zimbabwe's independence in 1980, I imagine she knew how it felt to be away from family.

As the hours rolled into days and days quickly transformed into weeks, most people, including my family, believed I was dead. When, later, I told Beatrice that I thought I would never make it out alive since my captors had threatened me with death during interrogation, Beatrice revealed that despite her efforts on my behalf she, too, feared that I had suffered the same fate as Tonderai Ndira, an MDC-T activist, who died only minutes after he had been snatched.

These fears were exacerbated by the fact that the state media failed to mention my disappearance at all. Some speculated that I might have been thrown into the Kariba Dam or some other place for wild animals to prey on my body. Stories circulated of a dead woman in her 'night clothes' who had been dumped in Kariba. My brother Cosmas told me later that he received many calls from people telling him about female bodies dumped in various places and lawyer colleagues were kept busy viewing every female body that was discovered.

Cosmas himself embarked on a dark journey that many would not even want to contemplate, gathering the courage and will to search morgues in Harare, committing to look at every female body. He believed I had been killed and wanted to retrieve my body for a decent burial.

What worries me is that Cosmas, even now, refuses to seek counselling and there are periods when he complains that he can't sleep. My nephew Vincent, my late sister Jennifer's second son, who worked for ZPP in Bulawayo as a driver tried to talk him out of the morgue search. 'Sekuru, I think you have gone too far, I don't think you will find mama there.' But Cosmas's mind was made up. He could not wait any longer to find out what had happened to me, believing it was time to accept that I was dead.

At Vincent's suggestion they began searching hospitals, but soon gave up. Many hospitals were empty and some were actually closed because in 2008 the country lacked the personnel and resources to keep them open.

Cosmas had visited several morgues when Ms Muchinguri told him she

21

had arranged a meeting with the Minister of Home Affairs. The search was abandoned briefly, with Cosmas intending to resume after the meeting. However, when he apprised the minister of his morgue search, he was told that he was looking in the wrong place.

Overjoyed, Cosmas believed the minister had not intended his words simply to stop the morgue search but that they revealed that I was still alive and that he knew where I was. A subsequent meeting with the minister was, however, cancelled when he made it known that he was angered by reports in social and print media.

Cosmas's next move was to extend his search to Goromonzi prison, 32km east of Harare. The prison was known to have a unit that was used by Central Intelligence Operatives as a torture camp. The family tried to talk him out of this, believing the mission was too dangerous and might lead to two members of the family being 'disappeared'.

The trip to Goromonzi proved futile, but Cosmas refused to be discouraged and made his way to Gweru, where many of our departed family members are buried, visiting the resting places of our paternal grandmother, our father, our two brothers, Robson and Canaan, and our sister.

My other brother, Peter, with the help of well-wishers and relatives, visited Apostolic prophets for information about my whereabouts. After 'seeing a vision' one such prophet dropped a bombshell: 'I no longer see her on the radar.' My mother went into mourning.

A further suggestion was that they consult 'an expert' in bringing back people taken by the CIO. The 'expert' requested one of my dresses – to date it has not been returned. On 10 December, Human Rights Day, lawyers and other human rights activists took to the streets to register their disgust at the disappearance of a defenceless woman.

Zimbabwe Lawyers for Human Rights tried every trick in the book in the courts and outside the courts and our borders. They provided all the necessary resources, both financial and material, deployed the best defence team and, immediately after I disappeared, assisted my brother Simon to file an application in the High Court against The Commissioner General of Police and others, seeking an order that compelled the police to investigate my disappearance and prosecute those responsible.

A number of communications and urgent appeals were also sent to the African Commission on Human and Peoples' Rights, to the Special Rapporteur on Protection of Human Rights Defenders and to the United Nations Human Rights Mechanisms, the Working Group on Arbitrary Arrest and Detention and the Working Group on Enforced Disappearances.

The fight in the courts had its own dramas. The efforts of human rights lawyers to establish my whereabouts were impeded by judges who were unwilling to hear the case. Some discovered that they were on vacation, others switched off their mobile phones for fear of being reached by the lawyers.

Friends and colleagues participated in media debates in neighbouring South Africa and the media there joined in the demands for my release, with the cornrow-plaited Udi Nakamela on SABC Africa becoming an instant favourite with my family when he launched a campaign to find me. The African National Congress Women's League's *Sisi* Tolashe was appalled: 'As women we are gravely concerned about the safety of Jestina Mukoko, the human rights activist who disappeared on the 3rd of December 2008. It is alleged that she was abducted by 15 armed men,' she said in a statement.

St Francis, my local parish of the Anglican Church of the Province of Central Africa (CPCA) in Norton, initiated prayer sessions with the family and encouraged members of the family to fast and pray.

Ironically, on the Sunday before my abduction, at a harvest function at the church, I had spoken about people who had been abducted in October and November. I was to meet some of them later in police cells and prison.

The St Matthew's parish in Mutapa, Gweru, where my mother and sister-in-law are parishioners, the church I grew up in and where I was baptised, dedicated prayers, as did St Peter's Parish in Mabelreign and many others that I am unable to list by name. Bishop Sebastian Bakare, as head of my church in 2008, participated fully in all these endeavours.

International organisations launched campaigns for my unconditional release and family, friends and colleagues abroad organised vigils. In Ireland, colleagues launched a campaign and initiated prayer meetings. A group of elderly congregants at a Catholic church in Belfast dedicated prayers to me on 23 December and the very next day I made my first appearance in court.

In many homes families prayed for my release and freedom after the information about my disappearance was made public on 3 December 2008. As a free person I continue to receive hugs and see an outpouring of emotion and prayers when people meet me and explain how they fasted and called out for divine intervention. I am humbled as I walk in Harare and people approach to tell me how they interceded on my part. At times emotions run high.

Raymond Majongwe, a fellow civil society leader, recorded a song dedicated to me at a time when no one knew my fate. In the song, entitled A campaign for Jestina, he prayed for heavenly mercies during the time I was detained incommunicado. When he tried to distribute the CDs to family members at one of my court appearances, state security agents wanted to know what he was handing out.

Majongwe wrote:

> I dedicate this song to the Director of the Zimbabwe Peace Project
> Jestina Mukoko, who disappeared on the 3rd of December 2008
> And many others who are in her predicament
> I say Lord God hear our prayers
> Jestina Mukoko Mwari muchengetei (Lord protect her)
> I sing a song
> I pray to God time has come listen to our prayers
> Jestina Mukoko please Jestina Mukoko
> Save her life
> Lord my God
> I pray to thee
> Jestina I know the girl
> Jestina I worked with the girl
> She was a marvel, she was a star, she was exciting
> Jestina and others must come back well, safe and alive

Francesca Mandeya, a civil society colleague with whom I share a totem, wrote a poem.

Jestina

Where are you Jestina?
Where have they taken you?
Those who woke you from peaceful sleep
In the wee hours of the morning
While you adorned nothing but a flimsy nightdress
Groping in the dark without your spectacles.

Where are you Jestina?
Are they threatening to end your life?
Are they torturing you, punishing you
For the truth you stand up for?
Stifling your free spirit and silencing you?

Jestina, where are you?
Wherever you are, I know you are brave and resolute
You will survive their brute force
You will be out of that bottomless pit

But where are you Jestina?
Aghh. Musatitorere MaDube Wedu! (Please don't take away
our very own MaDube)

Cosmas admits that the whole experience helped him realise the supremacy of the Lord. 'If after all we have gone through a member of this family does not appreciate the power of prayer then all I can say is something must be very wrong with them.'

CHAPTER
three ▌Detention

'Yet she emerged unbroken. That is the thread that runs through all of our honorees' stories – that ability to draw strength from suffering, the determination to not just advance their own lives, but the lives of others as well.'

US first lady Michelle Obama at the 2010 US Secretary of State International Women of Courage Awards

A few minutes after I was deposited in what I had taken to be a pantry, the door was unlocked and a woman's voice asked, 'Good morning, how are you?' Confused, I said I was fine. The truth was I was not fine at all. I had been snatched from my home and anything might happen to me, so how could I be fine? The woman was in the company of a man who did not speak. I could see two sets of feet from under the cloth that covered my eyes. The woman's feet were in sandals, her nails brightly polished. The man was also wearing sandals. The door was locked again almost immediately after the greetings.

After a while I could tell that food was being served not far from my room. I imagined the type of food it might be, since the country was reeling under a serious food shortage. Most food shops were empty and people were making regular trips to South Africa, Botswana and Mozambique to shop.

The key turned and the door opened. 'You can remove the blindfold,' said a male voice. With no further communication, the spout of a metal garden watering can greeted me. The man holding the can signalled that I should wash my hands so that I could accept the plate of rice and two boiled eggs that a big dark woman close to him was holding. The washing of hands in running water was particularly encouraged at the time because a cholera outbreak was ravaging the country. The outbreak, which was only contained towards the end of 2009, claimed more than 4000 lives.

'Hey, hey you are wasting our time. Hurry up, we have a lot to do, we do not have the whole day to attend to one person,' warned the woman. I doubted whether the food would go beyond my throat and refused it politely, feigning a smile and muttering something about a stomach problem. Almost immediately the door was shut again but not before the woman instructed sternly, 'Since you do not want to eat tie up your eyes.' I put the blindfold back on.

It was clear that I was not the only person in the place and I wondered how many others there were and how they had come to be there. I had no idea how I would get answers to these questions.

The man with the watering can was to play a significant role during my stay at this facility but until he did I felt as though I was going mad. There were times when I would hear strange noises within the facility and imagined that I was continually the subject of discussion. I think solitary confinement is meant to send its victims to the brink of depression. These delusions were not helped by the fact that from somewhere in the house, as long as the power remained on, loud music blared constantly from the radio or the television. I suspected the reason was that the sound was meant to drown out the cries of those being tortured.

Some time after the food bearers had gone the door was opened again. It was the woman who had greeted me earlier. I was later told that her name was Alice, although it was not clear if that was her real name. She came in, holding a plastic bag from which she took a black and brown tent dress and plastic shoes. 'You can take off the night clothes and put on this dress,' she said, and, handing over the plastic shoes, told me, 'You will need these when you visit the toilet.'

I was reluctant to put on the dress, which I guessed had been bought at a market in Mbare popularly known as *MupedzaNhamo* [where troubles end], which deals in cheap second-hand clothes, but eventually slipped it over my long blue nightdress. I removed the dressing gown and asked if I could use it as a blindfold in place of the dirty mutton cloth I had been given by my captors.

My dressing gown, a shimmery baby blue, had been given to me years before by someone very special. Once I started to use it as a blindfold it was no longer an item of clothing I loved and treasured, it became something I loathed. It embodied the scars of the physical and emotional abuse I endured. It stole my ability to see where I was and even to see the ground I walked on.

Parts of the dressing gown are now in tatters because whenever I wasn't wearing it as a blindfold and was not in interrogation it occupied me. I would draw out the small threads until all that remained in a patch were threads following the same grain. It was transformed into an item into which I thrust my pain, anger, frustration and anxiety. As a detainee, incommunicado, drawing out threads from the dressing gown was therapeutic. I would take my time doing it and it occupied me for hours. By the time I was done with a patch, beside it would be another patch, in a different shape, the stain of my tears.

The big dark woman approached my 'cell', her arrival easily identifiable as she dragged her feet. She unlocked the door. 'Stand up! Keep your blindfold on and follow me,' she bellowed, grabbing my hand. I did not know whether I was going to be thrown into a dam or into a fire but I followed her. Finally we entered another room in the house. 'You can sit now and take off the blindfold,' she said. I sat on a mat and when I removed the blindfold I saw seven pairs of menacing eyes looking in my direction, intensifying my fear. If looks could kill I would have died that instant. The eyes belonged to six men and one woman – Alice, the woman who had given me the dress and shoes. I had never seen any of the men before. I was sweating profusely and regularly gasped for breath. There was a lapse of a few minutes before anyone said anything to me after my escort had left.

There was an old office desk at each end of the room. I sat near one of the desks and the men stood, huddled around the other, which was close to a large window. The woman sat on a chair near me. 'Jestina, we understand you work for the Zimbabwe Peace Project and we want you to tell us about the work ZPP does,' came the first instruction from the one who was addressed as Mararike.

Trying to control my breathing I began to explain the core business of the ZPP. Mararike interrupted my explanation. 'Enough of the constitutional mandate of ZPP. What we want to know from you is the unconstitutional mandate of your organisation and do not waste our time.'

I was at pains to explain that I was not aware of an unconstitutional mandate but before I had completed the statement one of the men, who was not endowed with height, jumped from where he stood at the other desk, charged towards me and shouted 'We want to know the people you work with at Harvest House (the MDC-T headquarters).' My fear intensified as the short man's voice rattled the glass in the French door at one side of the room. Confused, I said the people I knew at Harvest were the same people they knew, as they were always in the news.

I was shocked, because I have never been a card-carrying member of the MDC-T or any other political party. Nor does my organisation work with the MDC-T as it seeks to report objectively on incidents of political violence. As the man approached me I saw that he was actually frothing at the mouth. Visibly angry, he yelled, 'Who is Joseni?'

I did not know anyone by that name, but another of the men was adamant: 'You know him, he stays in Chitungwiza, and don't act as if you don't know him.' Could this be a case of mistaken identity? I had no idea what they were talking about. Four years later I did, indeed, meet Joseni at a function at which then Prime Minister Tsvangirai launched his book, *In the Deep End*. When Joseni approached me at the function I was convinced state security agents were following me again.

The short man abruptly turned away from me, left the room briefly and returned, armed with a truncheon and a piece of rubber hose about half a metre long.

'Take off your shoes,' he roared, charging towards me. 'You think we are here to play with you. We do not have time to waste!' He put the truncheon on the desk in front of his colleagues and began to lash the soles of my feet with the hose. Initially I screamed as the pain intensified, but realising that in doing so, I was giving them satisfaction, I decided to endure the pain in silence. Instead of flowing out, the tears and screams stung the same body that was trying to release them.

In no time the short man was alternating with a tall man who smelt as though he had not had a bath recently. He used the truncheon, the more painful of the two weapons – the same length but with rubber coiled on wire. I cringed, winced and twitched before the weapons reached the soles of my feet. This type of torture, known as *falanga*, is the most common form of torture used in Zimbabwe because it is believed that once the swelling on the soles subsides, it leaves no trace. However, doctors are now able to use a colour doppler scanner that can detect the dilated veins that are consistent with this type of torture.

'Colleagues, give me a moment with Ms Mukoko,' pleaded Alice after a few beatings, and the men all left in single file. I got a brief breather and Alice moved from the chair to the mat close to me. 'This is for you, put it on,' she said, handing me a pair of lime green panties that looked like a parachute. I was wearing no under garments. I put on the panties and the men came back almost as soon as I was done.

Tucked in the corner opposite where I was ordered to sit was an imposing piece of furniture. Grey, just shy of two metres high and made of steel, it completed the décor in the interrogation room, which would also become my 'bedroom'. It was a gun cabinet. I did not see it open at any time while I was a 'guest' but I used its handle a few times to hang my panties to dry after bathing. If I stretched out my legs they nearly touched the cabinet when I lay down at night.

The short man, leading the pack, banged on the desk with the truncheon and screamed, 'Put up your feet on the desk'. I did as instructed and the thrashing continued in that position. Each of the beatings lasted about five minutes as my torturers caught their breath or alternated with each other.

Among the information my interrogators wanted was Broderick Takawira's address and mobile number, but I did not know them. All I could tell them was that he lived in Mufakose and, when the beatings became unbearable, I pulled a number out of the air.

The shorter of the two men preferred me to have my legs on the desk as this allowed him to beat the soles of my feet without bending. I was glad I had agreed to put on the panties and I struggled to keep my thighs covered. The foul-mouthed short man noticed. 'No one here cares about your legs, so don't waste your time and get in my way as you try to cover those legs.' The beatings went on for several hours, alternating with more questions. 'At the end of this you will reveal the people you have been working with at the MDC-T. We know you work with them.'

The day before my abduction I had presented a paper at a function to launch the 16 Days of Activism for no Violence against Women and Children, organised by the Women's Coalition of Zimbabwe. In my presentation I had expressed my concern about the huge number of women who had experienced politically motivated rape in the run-up to the presidential run-off and how most of these women still carried the trauma as they had no one to talk to for fear of rejection by their communities on the one hand and the loss of their marriages and reprisals from perpetrators on the other.

I had spoken about the widespread 'terror bases' established by Zanu-PF militia to punish those they believed belonged to the opposition. There were estimated to be about 2000 of these bases, situated in various buildings, including schools. Temporary in nature, they could be abandoned overnight if the militia had word that election observers had wind of them. As had happened during the liberation struggle, women were recruited as

31

maids, cooks and bed companions for those who ran the bases. The women were frequently abused in one way or another and I had expressed my fears about the number who might have been infected with HIV as a result.

I had also announced my intention to meet officials from the Ministry of Health to find out whether the ministry was aware of the risks to which political violence exposed women. It now became clear that the gathering had been monitored because among the questions I was asked during the interrogation was where I had found the figures I had presented at the Women's Coalition meeting.

Changing the subject, Mararike, who had been quiet for a while, wanted to know, 'how many staff members did you leave in Botswana when you went there? And, by the way, who are the two staff members who used emergency travel documents to cross into Botswana? '

He was referring to a period during the aftermath of the violent elections when, with most of the staff at ZPP suffering from burnout and secondary trauma, a decision was taken to have a meeting with therapists to debrief them. The economic meltdown in Zimbabwe militated against us meeting in the country because of the high costs and the unavailability of food in most facilities, so we resolved to travel to neighbouring Botswana with our two therapists. Like many Zimbabweans, I travelled to Botswana regularly to stock up on food. Holding the debriefing session there would reward the staff by giving them an opportunity to shop for the approaching festive season.

The ZPP had many contacts in Botswana because, with Zimbabwe in the midst of an economic meltdown which affected pensions and medical insurance, we arranged with companies there to address staff on available options in that country. We went in November, when, it seems, my movements and those of my staff were already under surveillance.

'Jestina, you are not clever, we have a whole file on you,' said Mararike disdainfully, pointing to a file on the desk. 'My advice to you is to give us all the information we need so that you can go home.'

The man with the watering can entered, giving me a break from the beatings and interrogation when he signalled that food was ready. I was feeling weak after the morning marathon. I washed my hands, hoping and praying the food was safe. The watering can made me think. Earlier, when I had requested water to flush the toilet I was given a similar watering can and I wondered whether they had two identical cans or whether the same can was doing two very different jobs.

The meal was Zimbabwe's staple food – *sadza*, cabbage and beef. It was not well cooked. Although I wanted to boost my energy I struggled to eat. Left on my own in the room thoughts began to flood my mind and lumps developed in my throat as I fought back the tears. Could this have been the sign that my mother saw? I regretted not paying attention to what she had said. What had I done to deserve this?

The interrogators returned from lunch with renewed vigour. 'Did a police officer visit your offices in June?' asked another of the operatives, now holding the file in his hands. I recalled that a police officer had visited the office some time in June 2008 but I could not remember his name and because of this their anger was directed at my feet. At one time the beatings were so hard I thought it would not be long before my soles cracked open.

The police officer, whose name, I was later reminded, was Ricardo Hwasheni, had come to our offices, claiming that he had left the police force and that he believed his life was in danger because he had detailed his experiences in the police force in longhand in a hard cover writing book. When Broderick Takawira had read the book he had found nothing incriminating and we told him so. Hwasheni had asked for money to leave the country but was told that the ZPP doesn't offer that sort of service.

'Jestina we have told you before, stop lying to us. We know the police officer received money from you,' said Mararike as if sending a signal to his colleagues to beat me. 'The police officer crossed to Botswana using the money he got from ZPP. You can't deny that because we know you are always in Botswana.'

Alice tried to play good cop, addressing me as though I was a toddler. 'Do you want to suffer on behalf of other people? Just tell us the people you work with and we can drop you off at home before dark.'

I insisted that I did not work with the MDC-T and was not in a position to name anyone. They continued to alternate interrogation with beatings until early evening when food gave me another break. They all left the room and shortly afterwards vehicles drove out of the facility.

Between washing my hands and receiving my plate of food I looked at my feet, which were swollen. I tried to eat the meal of beans and *sadza* but only managed a little bit. I asked to use the bathroom. Not used to groping in the dark, I got up and left my dressing gown-turned-blindfold on the floor. The dark woman roared and I nearly missed a step. 'You are asking for a serious hiding. You do not at anytime leave this room without the blindfold.' I hobbled on my swollen feet – the pain was intense.

The arrangement was that the woman knocked on the door of the room we were in from the inside and someone came and led me to the toilet. The door was locked and I got brief respite from the blindfold. The toilet window, which was always open, was covered with mesh so nobody could see in. From inside, though, it was easy to see everything that happened outside. It was dark outside, which, it being summer, meant it must have been about 19h00.

When I needed to leave the toilet I put on the blindfold and knocked. As I thought about spending the night away from home unaccounted for, vehicles drove in and I nearly missed a heartbeat. A rowdy group approached the interrogation room. The key turned and they were back. This time they came in with a man who appeared to be their boss, a dark-complexioned man with an Afro hairdo.

They had been drinking and had brought in the beer bottles. The beer was a new brand of lager, 'the Eagle'. The short man bragged as he lifted his brown bottle as though it was some sort of idol, 'You see because this is an important assignment, the boss is entertaining us. This is not our money, we are still to be paid.'

Now Alice asked me to move from the mat on which I was sitting so that she could stretch out, and in no time she was snoring behind me while the men continued with the interrogation. The boss wanted an update on what progress had been made and who I had listed, so people could be picked up to fill up the detention centre. Mararike filled him in. 'She thinks this is child's play but she will talk, I can promise you.'

'Will someone bring the black bucket full of water,' commanded the boss. For some reason this did not happen, but the thrashings on the soles of my already swollen feet continued. The group was then joined by the man whose sandals I had noticed that morning in the 'pantry'. I gathered that he was known as 'Guns'. He shouted at the top of his voice, 'Jestina deserves to be beaten up, when she was at ZBC she used to be very arrogant.'

Eventually they all left and I struggled to wake Alice. I needed to respond to the call of nature. She was surprised to find that her colleagues had left. She knocked on the door several times before it was opened and she led me to the toilet. The plastic shoes that had originally seemed a size too big now hardly fitted on my swollen feet.

'You should have just revealed the names of the people you work with, both of us would have been home by now,' she said.

The previous time I had gone to the toilet there were signs that many other people were also using it. I had also heard voices in rooms nearby. When I finished Alice did not lead me to the room where the interrogation was taking place; I was taken back to the one I had been in before the interrogation. A dirty foam mat was spread on the floor.

In the interrogation room where Alice had slept I had noticed a large brown handbag. I had assumed that it belonged to Alice, but later discovered that the owner was Concilia Chinanzvavana, an MDC-T activist from Banket, 95 km north-west of Harare, who had been abducted together with her husband some time in early November. The interrogation room was her 'bedroom' and she had spent the time during my interrogation in the 'pantry'.

Twenty-four hours after I had been brought to the house, whose location I still don't know, though my colleagues Broderick and Pascal suspect it may have been in Braeside, Harare, Alice opened the door and announced that it was my turn to go and bath. The water, which was warm, was in an old used paint container that should have been black but had splashes of white paint on the outside. I suspected this was the black bucket that the boss had called for the previous night.

Alice gave me a used tablet of blue Lux soap and there was a

35

squeezed toothpaste tube on the windowsill. I had no towel and there was none visible in the bathroom, so I would have to dry myself with the panties I had been given the previous day.

Before bathing I took advantage of the warm water to soak my aching feet. I could not imagine going through any more beatings, I did not think my feet could survive it. My eyes filled with tears. After bathing I used an age-old method that I had learned from *mbuya* Mukoko to moisturise my skin, though it doesn't work for the face. I wet my hands, squeezed the tablet of soap and applied the soapy water to my limbs. When the water dries it gives the limbs an artificial shine, though the skin is prone to cracking. I asked for some water in a tumbler and, with no toothbrush available, I dropped some toothpaste into my mouth before gargling.

Once I had finished I did not immediately knock to be let out but took some time to see whether I could identify any landmarks through the wire mesh that covered the window, but all I saw were two parked vehicles. It seemed that the cars that brought the interrogators had not yet arrived.

My thoughts were interrupted by a loud knock on the door. 'Are you done, you have been in there for a while now?' After blindfolding myself I headed for the door, ready to be led out. The 'pantry' was adjacent to the kitchen and the entire place smelt of hard boiled eggs. Within minutes breakfast, consisting of two hard boiled eggs and two slices of bread, was served, with a cup of tea. I managed to drink half the tea and eat a slice of the bread and one egg, less the yoke, which had turned grey. I suspected the eggs had been boiled the night before.

I had heard a number of people come in and dreaded the turning of the key, which meant continuing where my interrogators had left off the previous night. I heard voices and realised that the boss was there. I could hear my heart thudding away at such a pace that it threatened to break out of the covering of my chest, which was heaving and out of control. My brow collected strings of sweat and I was uncomfortable in my own skin. The room had suddenly become very hot. December is the height of summer and the small window was closed. I was not called immediately and the waiting gnawed at me slowly. I had decided not to put on the wet panties, but used them as a fan in an attempt to dry them and slipped them on as soon as I sensed the big woman dragging her feet towards the room.

'Now that you have had some sleep and know what we want, do you remember the name of the police officer?' I did not. The interrogation shifted. 'How do you get the information in your reports and how do you identify the people that you assist?' I tried to explain, but they were not interested in my answers, it seemed they wanted particular answers but I did not have them.

The short man questioned me about how the ZPP gets its information. 'Some of the incidents you report happen in the middle of the night and you get the information correct?' I responded that the people who provide information are concerned Zimbabweans who want to see the rights of citizens respected. He then handed me a piece of paper and demanded that I list the names of these concerned Zimbabweans. I said there were many of them and I would not know where to begin. His body language told me he was not impressed by my response and I thought I might be punished for refusing to write names as instructed.

The subject of the interrogation turned again to Botswana. 'When you travelled to Botswana who did you meet and how many staff members did you leave there?' asked Mararike. Tired of responding to the same question I held back a while then explained again that I had not met and did not even know the people that they thought I had met – if they existed at all.

The short man was unarmed, perhaps he was not angry enough to collect his weapons. However, he embarked on a strange ranting sparked by the perception that I was an MDC-T stalwart and that while I was detained others in the party would scramble for positions in the new government. 'While you are here, your colleagues in the MDC-T are going to be appointing a director of information because you have decided not to reveal the names of the big fish,' the man raged.

Mararike sat on a chair facing me, while the boss seemed to be expecting someone or something. He stood close to the window, his attention divided between the interrogation and what was happening outside. My chest continued to heave and I struggled, dismally, to control it. I suspected the reason was that I feared more beatings.

The boss moved a few steps towards me, pointing a finger at me as if addressing a child. 'I am not governed by the 48-hour or even the 96-hour rule. You simply have to follow what we want here or you go extinct. There are several others buried around here,' he added, gesturing at the surrounds of the building.

According to the old Constitution anyone taken into detention must appear in court within 48 hours or the detaining authority must seek a 96-hour extension for further detention of the suspect. 'No one will find you here even if they try, so you might as well behave and tell us what we want. There are two options – either become a state witness or go extinct. It is your choice,' raged the boss. I was very afraid. I knew that people had been killed in similar circumstances and the thought of that happening to me lingered. On one of the days after this interrogation I realised that there were people digging behind the interrogation room and my mind resolved that it was my grave being dug.

At that moment I made an undertaking to myself that I would try to fend off sleep so that if I was to be killed I would have the opportunity to look into the eyes of my killer.

The boss left the room several times and, although it took a long time for the truncheons to be brought in, the short man punched the desk more than once. The loud music and the banging on the desk were frightening.

As if trying to curry favour with me, Mararike, who was fidgeting in his chair, said, 'there is no hurting of the flesh today. All that is required is for you to give us all the information we are looking for.' But I was not the right person to help them.

As the day wore on it became clear that someone had been after me for a long time. They knew about the places I frequented, the car I drove, where I had worked and lived and the campaigns I had been involved in. They questioned me about the distribution of T-shirts and caps in my home town of Gweru when I was still with Radio Voice of the

People. We had run a campaign to publicise the frequency of the station so people could tune in.

With most radio and television stations controlled by the state, Radio Voice of the People offered an alternative voice.

In the afternoon, well after lunch, there were still no truncheons, but the short man continued to bang on the furniture and each time he did so I feared he might leave to fetch the weapons of his trade.

After supper Mararike announced that because I had failed to give them what they wanted they had no choice but to 'take you to our bosses, whose faces you will not see as yours will be tied in a sack. We have no control over what they decide to do.' He signalled that I must put on the blindfold. Before I did so I noticed that one of the men who had sat next to me in the car from home was waiting in the next room.

I groped in the induced darkness, trying to be sure where I was stepping and the door of a van – the type known in Zimbabwe as a kombi and used for public transportation – slid open. I was instructed to lie on a seat that was more like a bench than a car seat. There were a number of people in the vehicle and I could identify 'Guns' and Mararike by their voices. After I was asked a few similar questions to those I had been asked in the afternoon relating to my distribution of T-shirts I sensed that they preferred to talk about other things among themselves.

The drive lasted for what seemed close to two hours on a winding road. After a while the kombi stopped and there was some shuffling between it and some place. For a while I sensed that I might be alone in the vehicle and strange thoughts troubled me. Perhaps they were going to blow it up, or maybe they were making a huge fire outside to throw me in. I dared not get up for fear that someone might be close to the vehicle, and, besides, I was blindfolded. After a good 40 to 50 minutes the door opened, the ignition was turned on and the car moved off again.

This part of the drive was equally long and I was sure I was back in the same place because the radio was blaring. I was led into the interrogation room, where Alice was fast asleep. She asked, 'Where are you people coming from at this time? It is one in the morning.' I was not best placed to answer her, it seemed she was not happy being woken up at such a late hour.

As I sat on the mat that she had left free for me something hot gushed out of my body and I felt a sharp pain in my lower back. I asked to be led to the bathroom and, just as I suspected, I had my periods. When I was growing up my mother had taught me that monthly periods are a private affair that are not announced to strangers, so what should I do? This being the first flow I knew I could manage through the night and I did not think Alice would be pleased to be burdened with searching for sanitary pads at this ungodly hour.

The next morning Alice asked what my totem is. A totem is a form of traditional identity in Zimbabwe. Totems are drawn from animals or birds that families identify with. The tradition is so strong that a man and a woman with the same totem cannot marry as they are considered relatives. If, for some reason, they have to marry, a ceremony is held to untie the relationship. Remembering that I had heard that people could be killed by using their totem, I made one up. The logic is that if your ancestors are approached using a totem they can identify with they can open floodgates for tragedy to strike.

My totem is the zebra – *mbizi* in ichiShona, *dube* in isiNdebele, but I told Alice that it is a lion. 'That is the same totem as my mother,' she said, and began to call me 'moms', the street lingo for mother. The zebra is a majestic animal that walks with a certain gaiety in its step. The stripes, which are like fingerprints – no two zebras have the same stripes – look extremely beautiful in the blazing Zimbabwean sun. The zebra adapts to difficult situations, for instance, never losing weight even in times of drought. There are praise songs for different totems and most Zimbabweans love to hear their own. When I have done something good for my mother or the family she takes time to sing *'Maita Mbizi, maita varihowera, varikumasumbureru, gwara'*, interspersing the words with ululation and clapping with cupped hands.

There was no interrogation on the third day and in the morning I told Alice about the need for sanitary pads, hoping that she would deal with it herself. During the day I had to use toilet paper and frequented the bathroom more than usual because it was only towards early evening that a man brought in the pads and two new pairs of panties. The items were in a shopping bag from the upmarket store, Bon Marché. The next day the boss wanted to know, 'Did you get your parcel?' Anyone listening would have been forgiven for thinking that he had bought me a Christmas present.

My periods had not been due for another two weeks and I was experiencing a lot of pain, anxiety and the fear of not knowing what would happen next. Supper came early and I was told I was going on another drive.

This time I was taken in a saloon car with two men flanking me, my head on the lap of the one to the right. The drive did not take long and when we arrived at our destination the driver blew the horn and waited for the gate to open. One of the two men who were sitting in front went out and, after ten or so minutes the rear left door opened. 'Come with me,' came the instruction as the man sitting next to the door got out to make way for me.

As I walked, forcing my sore legs along, I thought that perhaps the 'bosses' had been unavailable the day before and had made time today. I went up one step and there was a change of hands on my arm – someone else was now leading me. The room I entered was carpeted and, after a few steps, an order was given. 'Sit down!' I prepared to go all the way to the floor but something caught me. I was on a chair. I was uneasy in this chair, just occupying a small space of its base, not trying to sit back. I thought about the threat of extinction. All my strength transferred to my mouth and, between gritted teeth, I prayed quietly. My torso was constrained between a table and the back of the chair.

The furniture in this new interrogation was expensive and the room was well curtained and more opulent than the first. Later I was to wonder whether a particular house on Enterprise Road in Harare, between Arcturus and Glenara roads might have been the place. Whenever I drive past it I get goose bumps and I always want to look in when the double black gate is open. There are always unmarked vehicles parked there, some of their windows tinted.

A new male voice instructed, 'Remove the blindfold.' There were ten

41

people in the room, five on either side of a huge pine boardroom table. Nine of them were men and the one woman there was drowned by the mound of lever arch files beside her. She was close to me and, as she perused one, I tried to see whether I could read what she was reading.

'Be careful with that file, Jestina is trying to read,' said a light-skinned burly man, the only one who had spoken so far. She shifted the files out of my sight. I could only make out the frames of those at the end of the table, it was difficult to see them clearly because I was still without my glasses.

They did not tell me their names, but the light-skinned man, in an authoritative voice, broke the silence, bellowing 'We are from the law and we are here to talk to you.' Four years later I found out the man's name when I travelled with him on a flight from Cape Town to Harare. In the arrivals hall our eyes met and he knew and I knew that we were not meeting for the first time. I asked a colleague I was travelling with if he knew the man, who had moved to the other end of the hall while we waited to claim our bags from the carousel. He was an assistant commissioner in the Criminal Investigations Department.

My hosts were given refreshments – tea, served in a beautiful tea set and a jug of water for the Mazoe orange cordial drink. A burly man wearing a loose white lace African caftan offered me refreshment, but I declined. On my immediate left were two fairly young men, one wearing spectacles. They were all smartly dressed and the one without glasses was wearing a black lace shirt. The woman's hair was pulled up into a bun, with a hairpiece that dropped to her shoulders. She was wearing a black top and slightly faded jeans that defined her curves. She stood up once or twice to search for a file.

The interrogation followed the same lines as the previous ones. 'We want to know the people you are working with in the MDC-T and we also want to know about the police officer who came to your office,' demanded the assistant commissioner. I still did not remember the name of the police officer and I made it clear that I did not work with the MDC-T.

The assistant commissioner continued, 'We know you met the police officer in your office and he came ready with your stated requirements of an identity card and a photograph in police uniform.' This is not how it happened. I had met the officer in Broderick's office and I was already holding my handbag and my notebook because I was in a hurry to get to a meeting outside the office.

The police identity card had been on the desk when I entered Broderick's office. As if to chide me, the assistant commissioner said, as though to his colleagues, 'Do you remember Jestina asking the officer, "*Wazvipira here kufira nyika yako* [Are you committed to die for your country]?"' The name of the police officer might have slipped my mind but I am sure I never asked that question.

Visibly angry in response to my denial that I had made the statement or that I had met the officer in my office, the assistant commissioner charged towards me, going around the table to approach me from the left. By the time he reached me I was shaking and I think I now know why people soil themselves in the face of a threat. He stood very close to me and I could swear he could hear my heart thud. 'She thinks she is still talking to the people where she is coming from who are not doing their job properly. Bring my stick and I will teach her a lesson.'

'It is unfortunate the people holding you are using kid gloves with you,' said the assistant commissioner. It seemed that I was expected to confirm all the accusations they had put on the table. The pain in my feet was no kid glove show. I could hardly sleep or walk after the beatings and I was tempted to lift my feet to show what had been done to me.

'Don't look at me,' he raved. It was difficult to ignore a threat that was so close and was hovering over my head, but I looked down, though from time to time I raised my head. A short, dark man brought in a one-metre long bamboo stick, but the burly man in white advised him, shaking his head from side to side and looking him in the eye, 'Don't do it'. He slowly moved away.

'I feel sorry for you because you are wasting your time and ours – soon we will catch them all,' swore the assistant commissioner. Although he did not physically leave a mark with the bamboo stick, what he put me through left a deep scar that swelled and took a long time to heal.

A huge, dark man sitting towards the end of the table stood to address me.

He banged on the table and the vibrations reached my end of the table. 'Uchamama [You will defecate], Jestina, when we are done with you.' I could not believe that these words had come from a grown man. What I know is that as a child if I had said something like that and my mother or any other adult had found out I would have been severely punished.

During my court appearance I would hesitate to repeat the words but Beatrice, my attorney, insisted that I do so.

'Where did you leave your child?' the man asked arrogantly. I confirmed that I had left Takudzwa at home. 'Is your son still at home?' the man wanted to know. My heart sank. Since I had been taken from my home Takudzwa had occupied my thoughts – I was, after all, his only surviving parent.

Distracted from the goings-on in the room, I wondered just what had happened to my son. The woman forced a thick needle into my heart: 'By not giving us the information that we require from you, what you have done in the process is to sign away an opportunity to unite with your son. Only an irresponsible mother does what you are doing.'

One of the young men to the left confronted me: 'There are figures that you presented at a meeting on 2 December, where did you get them?' I told him the information had come from the community-based monitors the ZPP deployed.

Later that night, back in the first interrogation room, which was now my bedroom, I knew I was in deep trouble. Would I survive two interrogation centres? I began to hum my mother's favourite hymn – number 106 in the Anglican hymn book.

Mubatsiri wedu Mwari,
Tariro yeduzve,
Mudziviriri munhamo,
Chivimbo narini
(The Lord our helper,
our hope and strength,
the one who deters trouble our eternal hope)

I managed just one stanza because I did not know the others well without a hymn book. However, when I did get my hymn book, when I was in

Chikurubi, I learned the words and now I do not need to look up the hymn.

Humming the hymn ignited emotions I failed to deal with. I cried myself to sleep. But also, somehow, the hymn brought me closer to my family. I could almost touch them. In good and in bad times my mother sings and dances to this hymn and I knew that since 3 December it had echoed many times both in Gweru and in Norton.

This feeling would later be confirmed by my brother, Cosmas. 'At times I felt sorry for *mbuya* Mukoko and *gogo* Dizha because they would wake everyone up with either hymn 130 or 106, leading them in prayer. One time I looked at my watch and it was 3am.'

I would return to the second interrogation office on three occasions. The second time I was interrogated by a smaller group, without the assistant commissioner. I was told that I had to write a statement when I was returned to what had become my 'home'. As it turned out, I would have to write three statements before one was accepted. In the third statement I was instructed to say that I had referred the police officer, Hwasheni, to my friend Fidelis Mudimu, who had handed him the money. It was all fiction, no money had changed hands. I also had to include in the statement the names of my late father and my mother as well as my mother's residential address.

On the third occasion that I returned to the second interrogation office a video was recorded in which I was asked to repeat what I had said in the statement.

The burly man informed me that I was being recorded in order to establish whether I would qualify to be a state witness. I wanted to know what that would mean, as the 'boss' at the detention centre had told me that if I became a state witness he could improve my living conditions.

The burly man giggled. 'It does not mean going home but rather into protective custody because in your case your friends will think you have sold out. Hwasheni [the police officer to whom the ZPP was alleged to have given money] is in protective custody. Harrison [Nkomo, a lawyer who would be a member of my defence team] and other lawyers have the opportunity to visit him.' When I later asked Harrison about the visit he told me that Hwasheni had been 'wearing a suit, holding a television remote control and wanted us to believe that he was comfortable, but his body language told a different story'.

That day, taking advantage of the burly man's good mood, I asked to use the telephone. My request was followed by a prolonged silence and the burly man, who seemed to be the only one talking to me, asked who I wanted to call. Looking him in the eye I told him it was nearly the festive season and I wanted to speak to my son. In fact, what I wanted to do was establish Takudzwa's whereabouts and whether he was in any trouble. The man's response surprised me. 'I hope you do not think we could be that cruel.'

On the fifth day of my incarceration I was in the bathroom looking out through the mesh wire window when I saw a Mazda 626 pull up on the gravel driveway and watched as Broderick was led into the detention centre.

Later that afternoon during my interrogation Mararike was not his usual self. He banged on the desk and shouted, 'You think we are children, but today I will show you we are not because all along you have been lying to us since day one.' I insisted I had not lied. 'You deserve to be punished and that is all I can say about your behaviour. For your information, the record has been set straight and from now on think hard about your answers because we know everything,' he said.

In his rage, Mararike stormed out, and my mind focused on just one thing, the truncheons. When he came back he was holding something in his fists. He came to where I was sitting, emptied his hands and made two mounds of gravel. 'I want you to kneel,' he instructed, pointing to where my knees should be placed. The mounds reminded me of my childhood. When friends wanted to challenge each other we would make two sets of such mounds, which we called a mother's breasts. The kicking of the opponent's mother's breasts resulted in retaliation and the start of a fistfight.

As someone who is socialised to kneel, I thought it would be a piece of cake. I was so wrong. The pain was intense, numbing. I drifted out of my own body and watched this woman from the ceiling.

Despite the pain I still could not name people from the MDC-T. I had not worked with them on any project. I did not meet with anyone in Botswana to discuss the training of youths. I still did not remember the name of the police officer and I did not give him money to go to Botswana. The interrogation went on for about two hours and the pain was unbearable, the small stones kept pushing up bruising the hard skin of my knees.

The interrogation team was thinning out by the day and, on that day, there were only three of them. I was saved when all three filed out to respond to a phone call. I remained on my knees for more than 10 minutes, not knowing whether they would be coming back, then I heard a vehicle leave and the 'watering can man' came in to relieve me. The gravel had left marks on my knees and I had a cramp. I spent the next few minutes massaging my knees. I cannot believe that people leave home to go to work where their business is to inflict pain on others.

Broderick, I was to learn when I finally managed to speak to him, had been interrogated in the same room in the morning and was punished for being conservative with the truth. After he was beaten the soles of his feet turned black – a discolouration he carried for several months afterwards.

After more than 14 days in this detention place the 'watering can man' brought me my meal one evening and left me shell shocked when he said, 'My name is Cosmas'. When he returned to collect the plates and have me wash my hands he spoke softly, 'But I am a better Cosmas because I know where you are, unlike the other Cosmas, who is getting desperate and appealing to anyone who might know where you could be.

'I hear the other Cosmas regularly making passionate pleas on Studio 7,' he continued before disappearing again. I was shocked that someone from the Central Intelligence Organisation (CIO), which, I had established when I overheard a telephone conversation, was responsible for my incarceration, listened to those stations that had been declared to be 'pirate'. They included shortwave Radio Africa broadcasts from the United Kingdom, Studio 7 of the Voice of America from Washington, DC and Radio Voice of the People, broadcast from Cape Town, South Africa.

I am still not sure if Cosmas was his real name and I am torn between believing he was deployed to be pleasant as a bait to fish for information and considering that he did what he did out of the goodness of his heart and hoping that the Lord blesses him. Once he gave me an old magazine, *Fair Lady*, which helped distract me from the nightmare that continued to unfold and without which I might have lost my mind.

On another occasion he brought me a Mills and Boon novel, whose title I never got to know because its covers were torn. As someone within the system he knew the effect of solitary confinement. One night, while on night shift, Cosmas said I could sit between the two desks in my room to watch the television in the next room. It was always on so loudly when there was power that it hurt my ears. It was during a brief loss of power, when the music and the television were silent, that I had overheard the telephone conversation that suggested I was in a CIO detention centre.

I declined the offer to watch. Being short sighted I have trouble seeing things from a distance so I avoided straining my eyes, but my ears heard every word. Thus I learned about the death of the then Zanu-PF political commissar, Elliot Manyika, who was killed in a car accident on 6 December and was interred in the National Heroes Acre on 11 December. I listened to the address by the president at the burial, thinking I might hear him mention a woman who had disappeared. There was no mention, instead he scoffed at the idea of intervening in response to the cholera epidemic.

On one occasion I asked Cosmas about the digging outside the interrogation room. He explained that the workers were digging for ants the 'boss' liked that came out during the rainy season. The explanation came as a relief and I did not reveal my fears to Cosmas.

'*Sisi* (sister), I hear you wear glasses and I have been told that carrots improve eyesight,' said Cosmas during one of his meal duties. 'I have carrots in my garden and if you like mealie cobs I can bring those for you.' He brought the goodies, telling me to put them in a drawer until the coast was clear, meaning when all the vehicles had left the facility at the end of the day.

One night, during another power cut, I overheard the operative known as 'Guns' educating Cosmas about the movie *The Transporter*.

... there is a driver who is supposed to take commodities and people between point A and point B without opening the goods or speaking to the people. He does this well several times but one time when he transports a woman he makes a mistake. The woman, who is gagged, requests to relieve herself and he allows her and the woman flees.

As I listened I got the sense that Cosmas was being warned about getting too close to me.

Late one night, long after activity in the detention centre had died down, I experienced real terror when I saw the glass door that separated my room from the television room being covered with a curtain by the short operative, who had to stand on a chair to reach for the curtain hooks. I wondered why it had suddenly become necessary for the door to be curtained. Sweating and sensing danger I sat up, watching intently. I thought the worst was about to happen and I wanted to see the person who was going to do it. He did not see my movement because the room was dark, as it had been during my entire time as a 'guest'. I said a prayer quietly and started humming an Anglican hymn – number 130:

Mukristu usanete
Inzwa ingirosi yako
Uripedyo pemhandu
Namata urinde

(Christian! seek not yet repose,
Hear thy guardian angel say;
Thou art in the midst of foes --
Watch and pray.)

Singing hymns always brought me closer to the family during the dark days and nights and somehow after singing I gained a bit of courage to face my tormentors.

For a long time, perhaps an hour, I heard people talking in the next room but the voices were low and difficult to catch. My mind went wild as I speculated about the reason for the curtain.

49

CHAPTER
four ▌Changes

On the evening of 22 December Cosmas brought me a plate of *sadza* and beans – meat had disappeared from our plates several days earlier. It was a significant date in Zimbabwe – a public holiday called Unity Day, marking the date in 1987 when the late Dr Joshua Nkomo of the Patriotic Front Zimbabwe African People's Union (PF-Zapu) and President Robert Mugabe buried the hatchet following the Matebeleland and Midlands massacres of the 1980s known as *Gukurahundi* (a Shona term for first rains that wash away all the chaff). They signed a Unity Accord, which included the incorporation of Zapu into what became Zanu-PF.

In his usual big brother fashion, Cosmas said, '*Sisi* eat up as quickly as possible, things are about to change here. 'His words drove away my appetite and when he returned I had not touched the meal. He was agitated: 'But *Sisi*, how come you still have not eaten, I have to take away the plate.' He collected the plate and that was the last time I saw Cosmas.

Three men I had never seen before came into my room and my heart started racing. One of them roared, 'pick whatever is yours and leave the blankets'. The other two men looked around the room as I picked up what was 'mine'. Since I had been given a dress, what belonged to me were my night dress, the blue dressing gown and the panties. Weird thoughts flooded my mind. People have a strange way of adapting to an environment and I did not want to be moved to a new place but another thought said perhaps they had decided to take me home.

The wall in the room announced the arrival of several cars, their headlights glaring off it. Some left the facility before I left the room. There was a lot of shuffling, indicating people in blindfolds being led out. I had learnt that when walking blindfolded you glue your legs to the ground as a way of detecting where they are going to land. I detected a number of legs moving in this way. I suspected the facility was being emptied.

In the morning Alice had lent me some of her clothes – a black skirt and an orange woollen top – so that I could wash my dress for the third time. On the other occasions I had just put on my nightdress and gown but this time she had insisted on giving me her clothes. Now I told them I needed to change into my own clothes and the big woman brought my dress, which was now dry.

Blindfold on, my possessions in my hand, I started the slow journey to an unknown world. Outside it was drizzling. In the car I recognised from their voices that I was squeezed between the big woman and Gatuso, one of the helpers at the facility. After a few minutes the car stopped and Gatuso opened the door to get instructions, ordering the rest of us to remain in the car until he told us to get out. Some 30 minutes later I was handed over to someone else, who took me up a flight of stairs to a room where I realised there were other people. A small child was crying, perhaps afraid of all these people in blindfolds.

A voice pierced the conversations and the crying of the child. 'My name is Peter Magwenzi and I am here to tell you that you are now at a police station.' Almost instantly someone shouted, 'Which police station?' I wanted to know if I could remove the blindfold but Magwenzi poured cold water on that idea. 'You will be advised on all that as time goes on; for now I want to take your details.'

He read out personal information for which he required confirmation. He then advised us that we would be taken to different police stations in Harare. He called out for people to lead us out down the flight of stairs and into a different vehicle from the one that had brought me here. This one felt like a double cab truck – there was very little space on the back seat and we were really squashed. Behind us, in the back, which was open, were Broderick and Pascal, among others. On my seat were Concilia, Violet Mupfuranhewe (with her two-year-old son, Nigel) and Tawanda Bvumo, MDC-T activists who had been abducted weeks before I was.

The truck was driven by an officer who seemed more interested in chatting with his girlfriend than in what was happening in the car. He was accompanied by a man I was later to learn was Officer Chibaya.

The first stop was at Braeside police station where Officer Chibaya wanted to check in Broderick and me. As we left the car Chibaya said we should remove the blindfolds. We sat on the floor in the charge office and began to catch up. We could not stop talking about the experience. Our conversation was interrupted when the officer in charge walked in. When Chibaya asked him to book me and Broderick in he was told I could not be accommodated because the toilets in the female section were blocked and the section was not being used.

When I returned to the vehicle I was shocked to see that all the people in the back were wearing blindfolds. I could not believe that in the middle of Harare's busy roads nobody seemed to have noticed this fact. For a long time after I was out on bail I would make it my business to peep into suspicious vehicles to see if anybody was wearing a blindfold.

Our next stop was at Rhodesville police station, where Pascal was accommodated. The female toilets at this police station were also blocked. At Highlands police station there was room for Concilia and me but I was there for only a few minutes before Chibaya and his colleague returned to collect me. The conversation we had just initiated was unceremoniously interrupted when a police officer called from the door, 'Miss Mukoko, please come with me.' As I walked with the police officer from the cells I nearly missed a step when I saw in the car park the vehicle

Jestina on graduation day with from left *mbuya* mukoko, cousin Beauty, brother Robson, cousin Molly and sister Jennifer sitting 1990

Late husband Herbert Dizha with son Takudzwa 1991

On the News Desk at Zimbabwe Broadcast Corporation 1994

Gogo Dizha, *mbuya* Mukoko and *mbuya* mukoko's sister 2002

MISSING PERSONS APPEAL

Ms Jestina Mukoko, the Director of the Zimbabwe Peace Project (ZPP) was abducted from her Norton home by unidentified people at around 05 00hours on Wednesday 3 December 2008. Ms Mukoko is a crusading human rights defender and a former broadcaster. One of the unmarked vehicles used during the abduction has been identified as a silver Mazda 323 Familia.

Mr Broderick Takawira, the Provincial Coordinator of the ZPP, and Pascal Gonzo, the Driver of ZPP were abducted on 8 December 2008 by 5 unidentified men who had forcibly entered the ZPP premises in Mount Pleasant.

We are appealing to anyone with any information to ascertain Ms Mukoko, Mr Takawira and Mr Gonzo's whereabouts to please contact lawyers representing them on the following contact details.

04 - 251 468, 04 - 708 118, 04 - 705 370, 04 - 772051

Cellphones:- 011 619 746, 011 619 747, 011 619 749, 011 635 448, 011 635 451, 011 635 455, 0912 257 247, 0912 218 754

Missing person's appeal for Jestina, Broderick and Pascal 2008

The dressing gown, nightdress, tent dress and plastic shoes worn by Jestina during her disappearance 2008

The famous plastic shoes 2008

Red van used to ferry the abductees including Jestina. Initially it had South African registration plates 2008-2009

Enforced Disappearances Protests December 2008

Jestina arriving at court December 24, 2008

February 11th 2009

Dear Juskine

I am deeply concerned for your situation and the situation of the other members of the Zimbabwe Peace Project.

I want you to know that you are not alone in this struggle and that we will continue to support you.

Sincerely, Ami

Mme Justine Mukoko
Chikurubi Maximum
               Security Prison
Chikurubi Prison Complex
Private Bag 7392
Greendale
Harare
Zimbabwe

A sample of thousands of cards received from Amnesty International
Supporters 2009

Receiving the City of Weimer Human Rights Prize with Takudzwa and co winner Sonja Bisenko of Serbia 2009

Outside the Catholic Cathedral in Belfast, Ireland 2009

Receiving the US Secretary of State International Women of Courage
Award flanked by then Secretary of State Hilary Clinton and US First
Lady Michelle Obama in March 2010

The Progressive Teachers' Union of Zimbabwe would like to join pro-democracy organisations and individuals in congratulating Jestina Mukoko for scooping the French Order of the Legion of Honour Award. The fight for a better Zimbabwe requires courageous, consistent and principled men and women. Jestina Mukoko has been a victim of an oppressive regime which has the presence of evil and a strong inclination to frustrate popular struggles.

As we congratulate one of Zimbabwe's finest daughters, we urge all Zimbabweans to marvel at Jestina Mukoko and rekindle the culture and politics of resistance which our forefathers have been known for. If our generation does not stand up to fight for a new order in our society, there is great risk of our children normalising the political and economic injustices which we are experiencing in contemporary Zimbabwe.

The constituency of teachers is a target for political persecution in the country. The unresponsive and lethargic bureaucracy of the Ministry of Education and its willingness to associate with forces of darkness has worsened the security situation of teachers. Jestina Mukoko's work as a human rights defender has great potential to deliver teachers from their oppressors.

As an organisation, we stand ready to partner with the critical mass of pro-democracy forces to better our society. **Congratulation our student, Jestina Mukoko, for morally using knowledge which you acquired from your poorly paid teachers when you were still at school.** We regret as teachers to find some of our former students who are now professors using knowledge immorally to destroy our society. Jestina Mukoko has refused to be such a graduate of education system.

Long Live Teaching!

Long Live Jestina Mukoko Our Student!

INSERTED BY:NATIONAL EXECUTIVE COMMITTEE

ZESN

Zimbabwe Election Support Network

Jestina Mukoko

NDJESTINA

Mukoko honoured in France

● From Page 23

of recruiting youths for military training with the then opposition Movement for Democratic Change. She was beaten on the soles of her feet with rubber truncheons (allegedly a favourite torture instrument of the regime in Zimbabwe because they leave no marks likely to be visible at later court appearances).

After three days she was handed over to another group of interrogators who claimed they were "law and order" officials. She was threatened with "extinction" if she chose not to be a witness to the alleged cases of military training. Prominent world figures including Gordon Brown and Condoleezza Rice demanded her release.

The Zimbabwe High Court ordered the Zimbabwe Republic Police to look for Mukoko. The order was ignored by the police who denied knowledge of her whereabouts. Meanwhile Mukoko had been forced to kneel on gravel for hours while being interrogated in an attempt to force her to sign a statement that she had recruited an ex-policeman to the supposed plot. Her medical condition deteriorated and she was eventually given medicine to treat serious allergies. She was forced to read statements on camera and pressurised to admit links to former policeman Fidelis Mudimu. She overheard someone say they were at the King George VI Barracks outside Harare.

She was eventually told that she and another abductee, her colleague, Broderick Takawera, were in police custody. She was moved around between different police stations and forced to accompany police on searches of her home and office.

On December 24 the State-run *Herald* newspaper reported that Mukoko had appeared in court in Harare on charges of attempting to recruit people for military training to try to overthrow the government. She had not been able to consult with lawyers. She appeared in court with seven other abductees, including a

Jestina Mukoko

72-year-old man and a two-year-old boy whose father and mother, Violet Mupfuranhehwe and Collen Mutemagawo, were also in detention.

In March 2009, three months after her abduction, Jestina Mukoko was released on bail. Her bail conditions required her to report to her local police station in Norton on a weekly basis and surrender her passport.

On September 21 2009 the Zimbabwe Supreme Court ordered a permanent stay of criminal proceedings against Jestina Mukoko. Amnesty International welcomed the decision, commenting that the charges were widely believed to have been trumped up by President Robert Mugabe's government as part of a wider strategy to silence perceived political opponents.

● *http://www.newsday.co.zw/ article/2011-03-28-jestina-mukoko-honoured*
http://en.wikipedia.org/wiki/ Jestina_Mukoko

Biatrice Mtetwa and Jestina Mukoko

Congratulatory messages for Mukoko 2011

The **LEGAL MONITOR**

ZIMBABWE LAWYERS FOR HUMAN RIGHTS
Fostering a culture of human rights

For feedback please email ZLHR on: info@zlhr.org.zw visit: www.zlhr.org.zw

11 March 2013

A newsletter published by Zimbabwe Lawyers for Human Rights for members & human rights defenders

COST: FREE

Edition 183

Distributed without any inserts

Hounded again

Joint CSOs' Statement on Criminalisation of Human Rights Defenders

HARARE, 08 March 2013-We, the undersigned Zimbabwean Civil Society Organizations, condemn the sustained and escalating assault on non-governmental organisations (NGOs) involved in civic education, human rights monitoring, public outreach and service provision by the State.

> ### 'Such harassment is meant to discredit civil society as unpatriotic and devoid of national interest. The relentless assault on CSOs and accusing them of several unfounded misdemeanors is to suggest to the public the existence of a wide-ranging conspiracy targeting the stability of the country and to paint civil society organisations as a danger to State security'

These flagrant, intimidatory and repressive attacks on civil society organizations and their leaders culminated in the Friday 08 March 2013 charging of Zimbabwe Peace Project national director Jestina Mukoko with contravening the Private Voluntary Organisations Act, the Broadcasting Services Act and the Customs and Excise Act. The criminalization of the work of civil society by the Government of National Unity is in direct contradiction with the letter and Spirit of the Global Political Agreement. It appears to us that the persecution of Jestina, who is not at anytime a fugitive from justice, is a direct victimization of an individual, who has been a victim of abduction by State security agents. State actions

against Jestina were condemned by the Supreme Court and her prosecution quashed.

We have over a lengthy period of time taken note and documented the intensive harassment and obstruction of the work of CSOs through intimidations, raids, issuance of vague and generalised search warrants, arrests, persecution and prosecution.

Such harassment is meant to discredit civil society as unpatriotic and devoid of national interest. The relentless assault on CSOs and accusing them of several unfounded misdemeanors is to suggest to the public the existence of a wide-ranging conspiracy targeting the stability of the country and to paint civil society organisations as a danger to State security.

Zimbabwean authorities, particularly the police, are fully aware of the role of civil society in a democracy but they have deliberately elected to mislead public opinion about our legitimate activities and continuously seek to impeach us on flimsy grounds.

We unequivocally deny all the insinuations and willful misrepresentations of our legitimate work. These allegations are meant to distract the attention of the public and international community from the important issues which the country is faced with. The issues include, among others, the full implementation of the Global Political Agreement, the holding of free and fair elections and critical institutional and legislative reforms meant to incubate the respect of the will of the people.

We hold the three political parties that form the inclusive government as responsible for the current crackdown on CSOs. Their failure to stop the unjustified attacks on CSOs, is testimony that they are involved in the coordination and implementation of the attacks and are not concerned with the challenges faced by those outside their ivory towers.

We therefore call upon:

1. the inclusive Government of Zimbabwe to immediately cease the harassment and criminalisation of CSOs and urgently take measures to ensure the protection of human rights defenders.

2. We further implore the inclusive Government of Zimbabwe to create an enabling operating environment for civil society in accordance with the Constitution, various regional and international norms to which Zimbabwe has bound itself through the African Union and the United Nations,

which clearly protect the rights of human rights defenders to associate, organise and carry out peaceful activities, and the right of human rights organisations to exist and be protected by law. In particular, the following minimum requirements in policy and practice for civil society to operate should be guaranteed: freedom of expression, freedom of association, freedom of assembly and the right to operate free from unwarranted State interference.

3. the police and prosecuting authorities to exercise professionalism and carry out their duties in a non-partisan manner and desist from the intimidation of human rights defenders.

We are convinced that these concerted attempts to criminalise and discredit our interventions in communities are wholly associated with the impending elections. We thus call upon the Southern African Development Community, as the guarantors of the coalition government and in line with its earlier summit resolutions, and the African Union, to exhort the Government of Zimbabwe to allow CSOs in Zimbabwe to operate without being criminalised, intimidated and harassed, as key prerequisites for the holding of free and fair.

Endorsed by
Combined Harare Residents Association
Counselling Services Unit
Crisis in Zimbabwe Coalition
Kubatana
Media Alliance of Zimbabwe
National Association of Non-Governmental Organisations
National Constitutional Assembly
Women's Coalition of Zimbabwe
Zimbabwe Congress of Trade Unions
Zimbabwe Election Support Network
Zimbabwe Human Rights Association
Zimbabwe Human Rights NGO Forum
Zimbabwe Lawyers for Human Rights
Zimbabwe Peace Project
Zimbabwe Women Lawyers Association

Police press charges against Mukoko

Police on Friday 08 March 2013 charged Zimbabwe Peace Project (ZPP) director Jestina Mukoko with contravening the Private Voluntary Organisations (PVO) Act, the Broadcasting Services Act and the Customs and Excise Act after she voluntarily reported at Harare Central Police Station.

The police charged Mukoko with contravening the Private Voluntary Organisations Act more specifically Section 6 (2) and (3) of the PVO Act Chapter 17.05.

Furthermore, the police preferred additional charges which included contravening the Broadcasting Services Act Section 38E (1) (a) for allegedly refusing or failing to register as a dealer and Section 182 of the Customs and Excise Act Chapter 23:02 for allegedly smuggling radios

and cellphones. A warned and cautioned statement was recorded from Mukoko in the presence of her legal team comprising of Beatrice Mtetwa, Harrison Nkomo, Tinvasi Mutangi, Tenderai Bhatasara and Tawands Zhuwarara, who are all members of Zimbabwe Lawyers for Human Rights. Mukoko denied all the charges and explained to the police that none of ZPP's activities were in any way illegal.

In her statement to the police she also raised the irregularity of the charges and more importantly that she could not be charged in her personal capacity.

Mukoko was then released into the custody of her lawyers after the interrogation and the police indicated that they would advise of any further action after assessing the docket.

①

Zimbabwe Lawyers for Human Rights article on Mukoko being targeted again in 2013

Timeline

...of Mukoko's persecution

3 December 2008
Mukoko is abducted from her Norton home by 5 unidentified men in a pre-dawn raid.

8 December 2008
Two ZPP employees - Broderick Takawira, the Provincial Coordinator and Pascal Gonzo, driver are abducted from their offices by unidentified men.

9 December 2008
High Court Judge Justice Gowora orders the police to search for Mukoko, to work with her lawyers and report daily on their progress, as well as to place a missing person notification in the media. This order was not complied with and the police denied that they had custody of Mukoko.

8 December 2008
At least 14 abductees, including Mukoko, located at various police stations in Harare by Zimbabwe Lawyers for Human Rights (ZLHR). The lawyers' task of tracing them was hindered by lack of cooperation by officers in charge and the transfer of individuals and groups from station to station. The lawyers were not allowed access to any of their clients.

8 December 2008
Mukoko appears at the Magistrates' Court. Officials from the Attorney-General's office fuse to inform defence lawyers of the charges until the matter was finally in Court. High Court Judge Justice Yunus Omerjee issues a final order directed to the Commissioner-General of Police and Chief Superintendent Magwenzi to release Mukoko and Takawira as well as seven other abductees held under warrants of detention, forthwith to Avenues Clinic under police guard, where they should be accorded full access to their legal practitioners and relatives. Mukoko could remain at the Avenues Clinic until 29th December 2008 when they should be taken directly to their Magistrates' Court appearance contesting their placement on remand. The Order was not complied with.

December 2008
Mukoko and eight others are removed from Harare Remand Prison and transferred to Chikurubi Maximum Security Prison.

December 2008
Magistrate Guvamombe rules that all the abductees should be allowed to see a doctor of their choice at Chikurubi Prison Hospital and that medical examination should be carried out before the case reopens on 5 January 2009.

January 2009
Magistrate Gloria Takundwa ruled that Jestina Mukoko must be allowed immediate medical treatment so that allegations of torture can be investigated before the case continues; the case postponed to the following day. The case of 7 other activists, accused of banditry, has also been postponed to 7 January 2009, pending a High Court ruling on their access to medical treatment.

January 2009
Mukoko's lawyers file a constitutional court challenge seeking protection and enforcement of the ZPP's executive director's fundamental rights, to have her released and not to be

prosecuted pending a full investigation into her abduction and prosecution of all those involved.

14 January 2009
The Supreme Court rules that Mukoko must be taken to a private clinic for urgent medical attention-an order which had not yet been complied with.

16 January 2009
The Magistrate's Court rules in favour of Mukoko taking her constitutional challenge to the Supreme Court.

20 January 2009
Mukoko is finally taken to the Avenues Clinic-in leg irons and under armed escort. After being examined and admitted for treatment, prison warders refuse to let her stay and against her will, against the doctors' orders and still connected to a drip, they moved her back to Chikurubi Maximum Security.

04 February 2009
The High Court rejects a bail application filed by Mukoko.

12 February 2009
Mukoko is finally taken to hospital where she is examined by doctors of her choice. Doctors are in agreement that Mukoko needs to be admitted to hospital. However, later in the afternoon, she is taken back to prison by prison warders.

27 February 2009
The Attorney General's Office summons defence lawyers and advise them that the State had changed its position and is no longer opposed to bail for the abductees.

02 March 2009
Mukoko is granted bail and released from hospital.

05 May 2009
Magistrate Catherine Chimanda revokes bail order and commits Mukoko together with 14 other abductees to Chikurubi Maximum Prison.

06 May 2009
Magistrate Chimanda admits Mukoko to bail on the conditions outlined when she was initially granted bail.

25 June 2009
The full bench of the Supreme Court sitting as a Constitutional Court hears Mukoko's constitutional challenge to determine a series of violations of her constitutional rights at the hands of state security agents. Chief Justice Godfrey Chidyausiku reserves judgment in the case.

20 July 2009
Jestina Mukoko sues for US$222 000 compensation in the High Court for mistreatment while in detention. In her claim Mukoko lists the then Ministry of State Security, Lands, Land Reform and Resettlement and its Minister Didymus Mutasa in his individual capacity. Co-Ministers of Home Affairs, Kembo Mohadi and Giles Mutsekwa, Defence Minister Emmerson Mnangagwa, Commissioner General of Police Augustine Chihuri, Chief Superintendent Magwenzi, Attorney General Johannes Tomana and Brigadier General Asher

Tapfumaneyi were cited as respondents.

28 September 2009
Mukoko wins a permanent stay of prosecution due to the violation of several of her fundamental rights by State security agents.

In the unanimous judgment by the Constitutional Court bench, Chief Justice Godfrey Chidyausiku, sitting with Deputy Chief Justice Malaba, and Justices Sandura, Ziyambi and Garwe, rules that Mukoko's constitutional rights were violated, and as a result her criminal prosecution had to be permanently stayed.

11 February 2013
Police raid the Zimbabwe Peace Project (ZPP) offices in Harare's Hillside suburb and seize several documents and other materials after searching the organisation's offices for "subversive material and illegal immigrants". The police officers who carried out the raid charge that there are reasonable grounds that ZPP was in possession of some articles which the organisation intended to use for criminal use in contravention of Section 40 of the Criminal Law (Codification and Reform) Act. The police also suspected ZPP to have contravened the Immigration Act by permitting some unidentified illegal immigrants to enter the country without a work permit and to have smuggled some undisclosed goods in breach of Section 182 (1) of the Customs and Excise Act. After the three-hour raid and search the police seize some documents and other items such as mobile phone handsets, wind up radios, files with donor information, political violence reports and DVD's. No-one is arrested but the police indicate that they are going to "study" the information.

06 March 2013
Police renew their onslaught against Mukoko by summoning her to report at Harare Central Police Station for allegedly operating an "unregistered" organisation.

07 March 2013
Mtetwa writes a letter to Detective Chief Inspector Run'anga that the Zimbabwe Peace Project's board had resolved that it would be represented by Dr Solomon Zwara, the organisation's chairperson and not by Mukoko, since she is simply an employee of ZPP and that she could not answer registration queries as she does not have board authority to speak or act on behalf of ZPP. Mtetwa also advised Run'anga that ZPP is a registered organisation and had provided its registration papers and Constitution to the police last month. Mtetwa also reminds the police that Mukoko has been a victim of State sponsored torture following her abduction by State security agents in December 2008, where she later miraculously found herself in the custody of officers from the CID's Law and Order Section at Harare Central Police Station, who have to date refused to disclose how she had come into their custody and who her captors and tormentors were.

Police Commissioner-General Augustine Chihuri issues a personal call for the arrest of Mukoko after claiming that she was on the run.

08 March 2013
Mukoko voluntarily reports at Harare Central Police Station accompanied by her lawyers where she is charged with contravening the Private Voluntary Organisations Act, the Broadcasting Services Act and the Customs and Excise Act. Police record a warned and cautioned statement from Jestina in the presence of her legal team comprising of Beatrice Mtetwa, Harrison Nkomo, Tarisai Mutangi, Tonderai Bhatasara and Tawanda Zhuwarara who are all members of Zimbabwe Lawyers for Human Rights. Mukoko denies all the charges and explains to the police that none of ZPP's activities were in any way illegal. Mukoko is released into the custody of her lawyers after the interrogation and the police indicate that they would advise of any further action after assessing the docket.

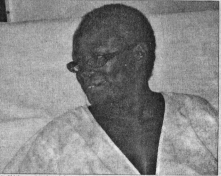

Jestina Mukoko recovering in hospital after her abduction in 2008

Timeline of Mukoko persecution 2013

Jestina with mother and brothers Peter (right) and Cosmas 2015

that had dropped me here. Chibaya was back for me, but why?

Chibaya filled me in. 'You cannot be at this police station. When we told the boss that we had left you and Concilia here he instructed us to come back and move you. You cannot be in the same cell as Concilia, she is facing the same charges as you are.'

Back in the car, and after claiming my belongings, his colleague, between the conversations with his girlfriend, suggested, 'I think it will be better to take her to Hatfield, they have better cells there.' Chibaya did not think so. 'I'm tired. We will drop her off at a police station on our way home – the closest is Matapi. Matapi, in Mbare, the oldest high-density suburb in Harare, has been condemned as unfit for human habitation.

'She is not to be seen by lawyers and relatives,' Chibaya told the police officers at Matapi, setting the rules. I was put into a cell with four other suspects and we haggled over the single blanket. As the last to check in I found a spot close to the door, which had an opening underneath which gave mosquitos free entry and they feasted on me in my sleeveless tent dress.

My fellow suspects wanted to know, 'What is your name and what are you in for?' I hid my identity during the night and told them I did not know what the charges were. One was suspected of stealing wet clothes from a washing line at one of the flats in Mbare. Another, who cried uncontrollably, was in custody on suspicion of stealing a mobile phone. The other two, who seemed to be unmoved by being in this cell, were suspected *mbanje* (marijuana) dealers and one of them had a terrible running stomach.

The next day two plainclothes officers signed me out to go for interrogation at the Criminal Investigations Department (CID) Serious Frauds unit at Ahmed House on Robson Manyika Street. When I walked into Peter Magwenzi's office a video recorder had been set up and the camera person, a light-complexioned young man – the same man who had recorded me at the second interrogation centre – prepared to start recording.

Officer Chibaya sat close to the door in Magwenzi's office. 'In this recording we want you to say the same things that you said when you were first recorded,' he instructed.

After the video recording I signed a warned and cautioned statement against my will. As if to reassure me, Magwenzi told me that my lawyer could later have the statement amended.

Superintendent Ncube, a police officer who had travelled all the way from Bulawayo, joined me just after I had signed the statement. 'You are now in the hands of the real police,' he said, but failed to inform me who had been holding me up to that point.

He had a search warrant for my house and also for the ZPP office. The warrant specified that the search was for weapons and cash. I had no problems with my house being searched immediately but to search the office he needed to inform the board members. In that way my colleagues would learn where I was.

I could only remember the number of one colleague. She was shocked and I sensed that she was failing to respond to Superintendent Ncube when he called her. It was only after three attempts on his part that she listened as he told her that she must inform the members of the board that the police would be searching my home and the office.

In the past there have been instances of weapons being planted on properties and, according to my brother Cosmas: 'For days if not weeks after you disappeared cars were on 24-hour surveillance around the premises. However, we just made sure we would never leave the premise unattended as my fear was that they might want to plant something on the property.'

Before we left Ahmed House several officers, who appeared to be concerned about my predicament, asked whether my family knew of my whereabouts. I gave one of them my younger brother's number which I knew by heart. She told me it was easier for her to use the landline in the office rather than her mobile phone, which could be traced. I felt as though I was on show, as one officer after another came into the room where I sat waiting for Superintendent Ncube.

Superintendent Ncube was joined on the trip to Norton by three other police officers in civilian clothes, one of them a woman. Cosmas, Vincent and Takudzwa were not at home. They had heard that I was at Matap and had decided to go there to bring food and a change of clothing.

My brother Peter, who opened the gate, was shocked to see me. When we drove in we found more people there – my mother, my mother-in-law and my niece, Jennifer and her daughter, Chipo MaDube and Golden were on a brief break having worked continuously while the house was full of relatives who came to console and comfort the family.

My niece and my mother were in the braai area tending some pots, my mother-in-law, who is partially blind, was sitting close to them. My mother screamed, called me by my middle name and also called me *mbuya*, meaning the mother of her husband.

Initially they seemed afraid to approach me, unsure about the group of people with me, but after a while they all embraced me as though we were at a funeral. I noticed my neighbours to the right sticking their heads out and imagined they must be thinking that my family had found my lifeless body.

My mother and mother-in-law started to weep hysterically in unison and, finally, I could not handle my emotions. All the tears and screams that had settled somewhere inside, threatening to drown me, burst out. The sight of these women ignited the pain I had endured, both physically and emotionally. The emotion that engulfed the house was thick, dark and piercing.

Officer Ncube informed everyone that he and his companions were police officers, there to 'search the house for weapons of war as well as cash'.

'Everyone will sit in one room and one of us will sit with you while the rest of us search the house in the company of Jestina,' said one of the other officers, laying down the ground rules. The search took a long time and, in fear of the police, no one called my brother Simon and his wife from their house a few metres away. They only got the message a few minutes before we left and tried frantically to stop the car on the road. The police thought they were mad.

I was given the chance to bring a change of clothing and picked a blue and red track suit jacket and pants to shield me from the mosquitoes that had had unobstructed access the previous night. The police confiscated an old computer and some documents and newsletters from other civil society organisations. They found neither weapons nor money.

Cosmas called my niece Jennifer's phone to inform the family that he had not found me at Matapi as I had been signed out for interrogation. Not knowing how to answer, Jennifer handed me the phone after telling Cosmas that I was at home. 'Which Jestina are you talking about?' he asked. I confirmed that it was me and that the police had a search warrant. I regretted not finding him at home.

I did finally see him when he visited me at Matapi early on Christmas Eve, despite the instruction that I was to receive no visitors. He was visibly troubled, looked as though he had not slept for several days and was too emotional to ask me anything about my experience.

A kind-hearted police officer, who could not understand why a brother who had not seen his sibling for 21 days was not allowed to visit her, allowed him in together with Takudzwa and my nephew, Vincent.

As he approached the cells, Cosmas, talking on the phone, walked a few paces behind Takudzwa and Vincent. Some of my fellow inmates were chatting with visitors, others were eating food brought by their loved ones. Vincent was holding the basket with my food and a police officer opened the gate for me to receive it.

'You can now go and speak to her from the fence,' advised the officer at the gate, signalling me to approach the fence. We began to chat and Takudzwa and Vincent tried to remain calm. Cosmas, who I could only see from a distance although I was itching for him to come closer, began to wail uncontrollably as he approached the fence.

Standing away from the other inmates and facing Vincent and Takudzwa, I was excited to see my brother, but I was stunned when, between his sobs, he shouted, 'That is not my sister, that is not my sister and I swear someone will pay dearly for this,' before he dropped and broke his mobile phone.

The police officer moved in quickly to walk him away before he had a chance to speak to me. In the 21 days that I had been in detention I had not looked in a mirror and I had no idea what I looked like. I knew that my spirit was still strong but I was upset that my brother seemed so disturbed by the sight of me.

| In Court At Last

O n the morning of 24 December, Christmas Eve, I was collected
from Matapi police cells by a woman detective, Maria Phiri, who
was accompanied by a male officer whose name I did not catch. Both
were in plain clothes.

I was flanked by two heavily armed police officers and was dazed
by the 'special' treatment I was receiving. Maria, busy talking on her
mobile phone to somebody who appeared to be an uncle, seemed to
be detached from what was happening.

Clutching a plastic bag holding my nightdress, dressing gown and
other personal items, I did not say a word. After a few minutes we arrived
at the Harare Magistrate's Court, which is known as Rotten Row. Another
police officer, in civilian clothes, one of those who had accompanied
me to search my house the previous day, rushed to the car and told
Maria to wait for a signal for me to leave the car.

The court grounds, guarded by heavily armed police officers, were a hive of activity and plainclothes officers, some of whom I had seen the day before, paced just outside the vehicle, talking on their mobile phones. Maria finished her conversation, announced that she wanted to catch a nap and lowered the seat right onto the lap of the officer sitting behind her, signalling for him to move over. That meant he moved towards me. We were now all perched on one side of the back seat. It was hot and increasingly uncomfortable, but nobody moved Maria.

In order to make some space and avoid too much contact with the officers I moved from resting my back against the seat to being suspended between the seats, holding onto the front passenger seat for balance. The police officers did not say a word. We were all suffocating and crammed in the position that the snoring Maria had put us in. We could almost hear each other's hearts beat and I was uncomfortable. I had not had a bath in two days. The other plainclothes officer had joined his colleagues outside in the game of pacing as soon as the car had pulled up.

As I tried to make myself comfortable and work out how I could have been taken to court without being informed or given the chance to instruct a lawyer, I saw a red van pull up beside our vehicle. In it were Broderick and Concilia. The van was full of people, but I didn't know any of the others.

The prisoners streamed out of the van to stand just in front of it as if on parade and I almost broke my neck trying to see whether Pascal was among them, but he was not there. While I was watching the goings-on around the red van, a plainclothes officer opened the door to my left and the officer who had been pushed up against the door to allow Maria to sleep almost fell out. 'She can come out now and follow me,' said the man who had opened the door.

The officers immediately rushed to flank me, leading me towards the underground cells. As we walked in a line to the cells, like cows to the slaughter, the mob that had gathered went wild. They all wanted to catch a glimpse of people they thought might never be seen alive again.

I was surprised to see so many people gathered at the court, but I later learned that the state-controlled *Herald* had carried the screaming headline, 'Mukoko to appear in Court'.

My brother shouted at the top of his voice, 'Tete(Shona term used to refer to an aunt) we are here for you, do not be afraid.' I could hear his voice but could not see him as people jostled to catch a first glimpse. However, in searching for him in the crowd I spotted Irene Petras, Executive Director of Zimbabwe Lawyers for Human Rights and I smiled all the way to the underground cells.

Simeon Mawanza, my Amnesty International colleague, remarked about my first appearance, 'Although it was evident you were not the same person we all knew I noticed a bounce in your step, which signified your strength.'

Broderick moved closer to walk in with me, whispering, 'These are the people who were 'disappeared' from Banket. There is a mother with a small child and a 72-year-old man.' I enquired about Pascal, but he had no more information than I had. I asked Broderick whether he remembered the name of the police officer who was the subject of my interrogation and he responded that it was Ricardo Hwasheni.

Within minutes of our arrival a troupe of human rights lawyers descended on the underground cells and we were all caught in the grip of our emotions. Dzimbabwe Chimbga, Otto Saki, Innocent Chagonda, Harrison Nkomo, Andrew Makoni, Charles Kwaramba, Roselyn Hanzi, all armed with pens and paper, could not believe their eyes. Here were the people they had been searching for, arriving from police stations in Harare with no explanation from the police, who had professed ignorance of the disappearances.

'Someone called me at around 21h00 last night. They did not identify themselves but announced that you people had been moved,' explained Otto, who with Harrison, for much of December, had the arduous and unenviable task of responding to any information about female bodies being dumped and checking on stone cold corpses, none of which matched my description. The group of lawyers divided up so that each of us could give a statement. The opportunity to talk to friends and colleagues for the first time gave rise to more outpourings of emotion.

The crowd in the courtroom had been here since our arrival in the morning, which, I think was before 10h00, and it was way after three in the afternoon when we streamed in after giving statements to the lawyers. As soon as we walked in, the public gallery, which was abuzz with conversation, went silent. In the courtroom I saw diplomats, civil society leaders, journalists and two members of the ZPP board – Fidelis Mudimu and Wellington Mbofana.

Tempers flared as people jostled to see the group in the dock and people shook their heads in disbelief when they saw Nigel, who, once in the dock, was attracted to the courtroom, and the prison official opened the door for him. He made people laugh and some choked with emotion just looking at him, but all that ended when the entrance of the magistrate was signalled.

By then I had my glasses and could see beyond the first rows. A friend Val Ingham-Thorpe, had noticed that I was battling to see and had signalled to Vincent to give me the glasses, which, luckily, he had brought with him.

Charles Kwaramba, a fearless young lawyer, stood up to address Magistrate Mishrod Guvamombe, asking him to release us. Fiddling with his jacket, as though to put the collar in place, he told the magistrate that the state was 'approaching the court with dirty hands'. The argument fell on deaf ears and the magistrate ruled that we must return to court on 29 December. Meanwhile, we were all to remain in custody. We were to be sent to Chikurubi prison.

As the court emptied, one individual was determined to talk to me. Sten Rylander, the Swedish ambassador, and he approached the dock. Before the prison officer could stop him he had shaken my hand, passing on, through his grip, a message of solidarity. I looked at him wanting to respond but my voice was choked by pain and nothing came out of my open mouth.

It seemed my story made a lasting impression on Ambassador Rylander, who, in an interview at the end of his tour of duty, said:

> The darkest experiences centre on the excessive violence and massive abuses of human rights that took place in 2007 and 2008. Strong memories from that time are when Morgan Tsvangirai was severely beaten up in March 2007 and when some of us went

looking for him around police stations in Harare. Also when Jestina Mukoko disappeared in November 2008 and when I spent most of my time during Christmas at Rotten Row Magistrates' Court attending the proceedings when she finally appeared again.

While we appeared at the Harare Magistrates Court on December 24 another court application was in progress at the High Court where Justice Yunus Omerjee presided and Beatrice Mtetwa represented the abductees.

CHAPTER six | Chikurubi

The men were checked in at Harare Central Prison, where initially we were all dropped off. As we sat in the reception area there seemed to be hive of activity around us, with prison officers being called several times to attend to inmates who had succumbed to the cholera epidemic.

There was a strong stench in the reception area, which had been sprayed to keep bacteria at bay. Word had filtered through the prison that the abductees were there and prison officers, as well as their 'A' prisoners, who had the freedom to move around, found excuses to come and view the actors in the horror movie of 2008.

It was I, who people recognised from my stint at the ZBC, who seemed to attract most of the attention. I, however, was worried about Broderick and the other men who would remain there, as well as about Nigel, who had to be restrained from playing freely in the recently sprayed reception area.

Along with the rest of the women, most of them MDC-T activists, I was integrated into the prison system through the Chikurubi female section. We arrived quite late on 24 December because our transport had to collect maize meal for the prison officers' food handouts, the *Bacossi*. Because of the desperate economic situation at the time, government officials were given food as it was not readily available in shops and, even if it was, in view of inflation few civil servants were not able to afford it.

As soon as we arrived, after an intensive search, which included parading our naked behinds to show that no items were hidden there, we were given new green uniforms, some still with the threads not cut. There were several plates of stone-cold *sadza* and *bonongwe*, a traditional vegetable and a favourite among some of us. Each inmate received two grey blankets and we were accommodated in the receiving cell – starkly different from the cells at Matapi police station.

Like the surrounding cells, it was locked and there were no toilets inside. The only piece of furniture was a yellow 20-litre plastic container with the top cut off to be used as a makeshift toilet for the night. The edge was rough and uncomfortable and it was inhumane to make us use it while others watched, even if we were all women. We agreed that the container would only be used for urine but the call of nature determined the pace. The next day Violet had a running tummy, which she relieved in plastic bags which were placed outside the room through the window for disposal in the morning.

Back in the cell with my fellow prisoners I regained my composure after the trauma in court. Many of them had been detained incommunicado for longer than I had, some having been abducted in October and some early in November. It had been a long day, but it was not easy to fall asleep. The other women were all from the same area and they caught up on how each had heard about the disappearance of the others.

One of the people I met at Chikurubi was Pieta Kaseke, who is related to Ricardo Hwasheni. She told me that Hwasheni had been kidnapped at a traffic light in Harare and his mother did not know where he was. Pieta, like all the other abductees except Audrey Zimbudzana, was a staunch MDC-T activist. This was the first time I had met any of them but I was linked to them in the charges. Pieta and Concilia's husband, Emmanuel Chinanzvavana, were supposed to be the people I had worked with.

I learned that Pieta, Violet, Nigel and *sekuru* Chiramba had been taken in one vehicle when they were abducted. Pieta and Violet provided a bit of laughter. 'While some of us were thinking about where they were taking us, *sekuru* Chiramba kept asking if the captors were ready to fill him in on his crime, and this he did several times, even after they yelled for him to shut up.' *Sekuru* Chiramba is a bold character with a great sense of humour. A retired police officer, he knows what is expected of an arresting officer. He had yelled so loudly when he was abducted that his neighbours heard him. This saved Concilia on that day, but she was later tracked down and waylaid near Harare, with both her husband and Violet's husband, Collen, as well as Tawanda Bvumo, who was driving them. Audrey Zimbudzana, who was in a relationship with a soldier from the military intelligence, was strangely, kidnapped right in front of her boyfriend.

Violet, aware that, as an MDC-T activist, she might be targeted for abduction, had gone to a neighbour's house, leaving Nigel and his five-year-old brother, Allan, at home. The captors played with the minds of the children. The year 2008 was a year of desperation and even children knew that food was hard to come by. The captors pretended to be selling beans and the children blindly led them to their mother. While Violet and Nigel were taken away, Allan was left with the neighbours and was later taken care of by Violet's mother.

Initially Violet, Pieta and *sekuru* Chiramba were taken into police custody and were then told they had been released and would be driven to Banket. They spent the day at a shopping centre, where they were instructed to remain in the car and told not to interact with anyone.

On what was supposed to be the drive back to Banket, their vehicle was 'waylaid' and they found themselves in incommunicado detention. Violet, Pieta and, for some time, *sekuru* Chiramba, were at the same detention centre – a different one from the place where Concilia, Broderick, Collen, Emmanuel, Pascal and I were detained.

The three of them, Nigel and other activists from Banket, Terry Musona and Fanny Tembo, who were alleged to have turned state witnesses, albeit against their will, spent the days and nights in the same room and were frequently assaulted while the others were forced to watch. Nigel endured whipping with a fanbelt on his tiny, fragile and still growing back, as a way of extracting information from Violet, who was accused of recruiting her brother, who is in Zambia, for training in acts of sabotage, terrorism and overthrowing a constitutionally elected government.

'I am not trying to compare situations but mine was a difficult experience with a child and to watch him being whipped was so painful,' Violet said. 'When Nigel slept I was relieved because I knew for a while he would not ask for anything. They would shout whenever Nigel asked for food and even if he wanted to use the toilet they would tell me to train him,' she remembered, and I noticed her eyes well up.

Audrey had been in the same detention centre as we were, but described a different world. She was not physically abused and spoke about sharing a bed with Alice, who had shared the room with me for a while but had then just disappeared. I would see her during the day and at night before everyone went to sleep.

The next day I finally got to have a bath – the police cells had had no bathing facilities. During a drill the following morning we were a spectacle and, as in all the other places in which I had been, I was the centre of attention. Prison officers and inmates alike streamed to the Female section to see Jestina Mukoko, the former Zimbabwe Broadcasting Corporation news anchor. For most of the morning we underwent the formalities of being admitted to the prison. We were weighed and all other details were recorded. A few days before 3 December I had been worried about my weight, which was 80kg. On this day I weighed a mere 52kg.

We remained in the receiving cell for three nights and three days. On Christmas day we saw a different side of the female prison. Inmates were allowed to put on earrings and apply make-up but of course they were not allowed access to these items, so the women became creative. Some were excellent hair stylists and, in the difficult economic climate, some prison officers relied on them to create trendy but inexpensive hairdos, some of which required hair extensions. The extensions were packaged with golden straps, which the inmates coiled for earrings. They ground different coloured bricks to make face powder for a matte finish and used black rubber as eyeliner for their eyes.

They looked splendid in their clean dresses – green for those on remand, and yellow for those convicted. The only mirror in the female section was in the receiving cell and we marvelled to watch them sprucing in preparation for visits later. The mirror was a no-go area for inmates, so we kept an eye out for the warders making their way to our cell.

The prison authorities only allowed two of the more than 15 people who came to visit me and when I saw Takudzwa I sobbed so bitterly that he spent the 20 minutes we were allowed trying to console me. 'Mama, please don't cry. You don't know how happy we all are to see you – this has turned out to be the best Christmas present ever,' he said, fighting back his own tears. Takudzwa had, I learned, at the last moment turned down an invitation to go away for Christmas. Dr Sanyama who he was living with at the time, would later tell me that he had asked to go to Norton to pick up some clothes for the trip but when he got there he had called to inform her that he had a strange feeling that he was about to see me and therefore could not go on the trip.

The prison officer who was overseeing the visit threatened me several times: 'I can get them to leave if you continue to cry.' She clearly had no understanding of my situation – I was no ordinary inmate, I had spent 21 days detained at a secret location where I was tortured and threatened with extinction. I ignored the officer and Takudzwa continued to comfort me, wiping away my tears.

On 26 December Audrey, a nurse, played midwife to an inmate who had gone into labour. She delivered a healthy baby boy. One of the hairstylists hinted as she plaited Concilia's hair that we might be moving soon. Other prisoners, she said, had been cleaning cells at the maximum security prison, blankets had been moved and light bulbs fitted.

On that day, too, we were allowed to receive visitors. *Mbuya* Mukoko was unable to join my mother-in-law and Vincent for the visit because she had not brought her identity documents and the officials at the gate refused to allow her in. *Gogo* Dizha took advantage of the visit to speak to the officer on duty while she waited to see me. As I walked into the office where I was meeting my visitors the officer announced, 'Your mother-in-law says you are special, we should look after you.' I was touched and could not hold back my tears. 'If you continue crying I will have no choice but to end this visit,' said the officer. Somehow this statement made me even more emotional.

After the visit I was summoned to the office of the officer in charge, a Mrs Chifodya, together with all the other fellow abductees now turned inmates. Lawyers Alec Muchadehama and Roselyn Hanzi were in the office. They had come to check whether the prison officials had complied with Justice Omerjee's order. They had discovered that the prosecution intended to appeal to the Supreme Court to have the order rescinded, which was why we had not been checked into the private hospital. The lawyers asked Mrs Chifodya to leave us, as is required by law, to facilitate unhindered consultation.

'The law is very clear that when lawyers take instructions from their clients you are supposed to be in eyeshot and not earshot,' said Alec. Mrs Chifodya continued to fidget at her desk. 'I suggest you get comfortable with me because I am not about to leave this office for any reason as long as these inmates are here,' she said.

On 27 December the receiving cell was locked earlier than usual and there seemed to be a lot of activity, which was confusing. Before dark, however, the door was unlocked again and all of us, except Violet and Nigel, were called out.

A white Mazda single-cab truck was waiting at the gate. Mrs Chifodya instructed us to get into the back of the vehicle. Nobody told us where we were going and we dared not ask. I was afraid we might be taken back to the detention centre and disappear again. The vehicle went through several gates that opened as it approached and closed immediately afterwards.

The journey ended in a courtyard with high walls and we were led through heavy wooden doors. The two people leading us were important here, prison officers saluted them all the way. We were taken up two flights of stairs to the top floor. Eight single cells lined one side of the floor and there was a secured place for the prison officer on duty. This was the Chikurubi Maximum Security Prison, where I was to remain for the next 50 days of my incarceration. Another 18 days I spent in hospital, under guard. I was convinced that the large overbearing walls had ice in them as the cells were freezing, even on very hot days.

There were piles and piles of blankets available. Some we rolled up to make the concrete bed more comfortable and one was turned into a pillow. At the end of the bed was a toilet that did not flush – there had apparently been no running water in the prison for some time. Inmates from the female section fetched water from wells and boreholes sunk by international organisations like the International Committee of the Red Cross and brought it in buckets to the maximum security prison twice a day.

I had a 20-litre container that was always filled with water. In order to bath, which I did before the cell doors were opened at 7h00 each morning, I straddled the toilet bowl so the water flowed into it. This also helped to clean the bowl. The prison guards were known as 'mbuya' and 'sekuru', which means grandmother and grandfather. I could not understand why they wanted to be addressed in this way and could not bring myself to use the terms.

The day after we arrived two high-ranking prison officers spelt out the rules and regulations. 'You are only allowed 30 minutes a day out of your cells to stretch in the courtyard.' Initially the attitude of the prison officers in maximum security was very different from that of those in the Women's Prison, who were quite pleasant. These seemed to be women on a mission and they wanted us to feel it. In time, however, while a few remained uncompromising, some thawed and developed a liking for us. It was they who alerted us to the fact that security had been beefed up, with operatives coming in disguised as prison warders.

Before the instruction that we were only allowed out for 30 minutes a day had sunk in, the officer in charge of the prison visited with his entourage. I was the only person in the courtyard at the time, which gave me the opportunity to follow their conversation.

One of the more junior officers explained about the 30-minutes-a-day rule but the officer in charge declared that we should be allowed in the courtyard from the time the cells were unlocked in the morning until lock-up in the afternoon.

CHAPTER
seven | Prosecution Or Persecution?

O n our way to court on 29 December the red van passed through the female section where we picked up Violet and Nigel. Nigel was surprised to see all of us in leg irons and handcuffs. He hopped into the van, and made the drive to the court light, cracking jokes all the way.

One of the senior female officers, who was eating her breakfast in the car, offered Nigel some homemade bread. 'If you want to give me bread you better give me proper bread because I do not eat this other homemade type that you people eat,' he said, and we were all in stitches. In a few days he had already learnt about the lifestyle of the prison officers.

We were packed like sardines since six more people, another group of abductees, had been added. Gandhi Mudzingwa, Kisimusi Dlamini, Chinoto Zulu, Andrrison Manyere, Garutsa Mapfumo and Regis Mujeyi were charged with bombing various police stations, railway lines and bridges and engaging in acts of banditry, insurgency, sabotage or terrorism.

They were also charged with contravening section 23 of the Criminal Law (Codification and Reform) Act, which carries a potential death sentence in the event that they were convicted.

'As head of security at the MDC-T, don't you think I should have known you before you started recruiting for us,' enquired Dlamini, looking me directly in the eye and fiddling with his handcuffs. Until his appearance in court the previous day the two of us had never set eyes on each other. His remark broke the ice and both prisoners and officers burst out laughing.

The van was delayed briefly as officers waited for two vehicles from the Zimbabwe Republic Police Support Unit, which provides armed protection for government officials and also responds to riots. *Sekuru* Chiramba explained that its other role was to provide an escort when dangerous criminals were being transported.

'Our driver is actually committing a crime by creating such a huge gap between this vehicle and the other escort vehicle,' he chuckled and, before long, the other vehicle blew its horn for the red van to reduce speed and narrow the gap. When we arrived in court we found that Pascal Gonzo was there too, along with another batch of abductees, all of them opposition activists.

The criminal charges were read out to us for the first time since we had been abducted. We were all charged with contravening section 24(a) of the Criminal Law (Codification and Reform) Act. The allegations were that we recruited or attempted to recruit individuals for training in banditry, insurgency, sabotage or terrorism to overthrow a constitutionally elected government.

The person I was accused of recruiting was Hwasheni. A single police officer in a period of more than six months! My relatives and friends found this accusation ludicrous. What surprised me was the fact that the beneficiary of our activities was supposed to have been Morgan Tsvangirai, but Tsvangirai was not in the dock with his so-called accomplices. Broderick, Pascal and I had no connection with the large group of opposition activists apart from our work monitoring and documenting politically motivated human rights violations.

It was common during my stay in Chikurubi Prison that we would leave

71

very early for court, but the proceedings would only start well after 14h00. The reason, I would learn from a relative who had met informally with one of the magistrates, was that it was policy not to allow human rights attorneys too much time to argue their case in case the argument was persuasive enough to sway the magistrate 'to make a decision that you will live to regret. The best is to give them very little time and postpone to the next day.'

Our lawyers learnt that Pascal and Tawanda Bvumo were to be charged with assisting the perpetrators of crimes after the crimes had been committed. This is an offence in terms of section 206 (a) and (b) of the Criminal Law (Codification and Reform) Act. Should they be convicted, they risked being sentenced to life imprisonment.

In his ruling, Magistrate Guvamombe ordered that all the abductees should be examined by doctors of their choice at Chikurubi. He refused to allow them to be taken to the Avenues Clinic. Our trial was postponed to 5 January 2009 but Pascal Gonzo's and Bvumo's was postponed until the next day.

Back at the prison, officers rounded us up, shackled us and took us to the prison hospital, where doctors examined us in the presence of the officers, who refused to give us privacy. The hospital did not have equipment to facilitate proper examinations, but I was given tablets that helped ease my aching feet and allowed me to sleep after a long time of living with the pain.

The following day, Magistrate Guvamombe ordered the release of both Pascal and Bvumo, but the clerk of the court was prevented from processing warrants of liberation by Florence Ziyambi from the Attorney General's office, who informed the magistrate that the state intended to appeal his decision. Nigel and his mother were moved from the female section of Chikurubi to join us in the maximum security section.

As a coping mechanism in prison I used the length of time spent by fellow human rights defenders to prepare myself physically and spiritually. Jenni Williams and Magodonga Mahlangu of the Women of Zimbabwe Arise had been held for 37 days. When I passed that mark I focused on fellow journalist Luke Tamborinyoka, who was incarcerated for 71 days.

Prison Life

The prison warders were provided with mealie meal but in order to get other types of food like meat or wheat for bread they walked long distances to surrounding farms to trade the mealie meal for meat – in most cases pork – and wheat to improve the diet of their families.

Some came to work at night after walking for hours in search of these products, arrived at work exhausted and announced as soon as they walked in that they were going to sleep. They told us this because they knew that the majority of us lay awake for long hours and could therefore hear footsteps approaching the top floor. Obviously we did not extend this benefit to all the warders, only to those we considered our friends.

The cell was locked from the outside, so the supervisor could walk in on the officer on duty at anytime. We allowed those who were good to us to enjoy their rest while we played guard and warned them of impending danger. There were those, though, who we believed to be spying on us or who called us all sorts of names. Rather than use our names some chose to call us by the colour of the dresses we wore –'*magreen*' (those in green dresses). We ceased to be human. The institution reduced us to a number. I was '723 of 2008' meaning female prisoner number 723 of 2008 and my identity was lost in so many ways within the high walls of the prison.

Some of the warders joined in when we appealed to the heavens for divine intervention, singing gospel hymns across the high cold walls that separated us, and also joined us in prayer. Nigel, not wanting to be left out, would request his favourite song, '*Isu tapiwa mumwe mukana zve wekuti timunamate* (We have been accorded another chance to praise Him)'.

One Saturday our singing and dancing in the courtyard with the officers on duty was so loud that our male counterparts on the other side of the prison wanted to know what we were celebrating. On that particular day the officers were so into the singing that they delayed locking us up for the night.

We built good relationships with some of the officers, to the extent that they confronted my family whenever they felt they had brought insufficient food. Some spoke about their boyfriends and partners, hoping to get advice. Takudzwa, taking advantage of these connections, would slip into their hands small pieces of paper containing Bible verses for me, which they would pass on later. The cordial relationships also meant that for a while my mother-in- law, who was partially visually impaired,was allowed to be taken by car close to the cells. However, this was stopped when security was increased.

Bishop Ancelimo Magaya and his wife fed me both spiritually and physically. I had known little about them before I was abducted but when I was incarcerated Bishop Magaya, who is visually impaired, walked the long distance between the gate and the prison just to ensure that he prayed with me.

Dreadlocked Simbarashe Moyo, then chairperson of the Student Solidarity Trust, came nearly every day to ensure that we were fed. I saw him come in one day when I was in the visiting booth and, despite being male, he had all the food packed neatly in an empty bread crate which he balanced on his head as a woman would.

My family, too, fed me fresh hot food daily and, because I did not eat prison food, some of the officers asked me to collect my ration, which they would pack and take home, where they garnished the salt-less, oil-less green vegetables. This was a clear indication that the situation was desperate in the country for most Zimbabweans, even those who were employed.

If an excess of food was delivered from outside we would share it with fellow prisoners and give what was left over to the warders, whose desperate situation was reflected not only in their hunger but in their torn and faded uniforms and shoes repaired so often that some looked like patchwork quilts. If they removed their shoes while we sat in the courtyard the holes in their socks were evident.

We were in separate cells at night and during other lock-up times and we shared the floor with two other women – Rosemary, fondly known as MaKhumalo, and MamNkandla, both of whom were on death row. MaKhumalo, who was in for armed robbery, insisted she had been set up. Rosemary, who was like a mother to me, pleated my dresses with knife pleats she had learnt to make without the use of an iron and taught me the art of survival in that cold environment.

She also crafted beautiful objects, bringing a large bag from her cell to the courtyard where we all spent most of our days. Her clever fingers worked shining pieces of paper from empty potato chip packets that had been cleaned and cut into neat strips. I watched with interest as she made objects from picture frames to toothbrush holders. I still use one of those toothbrush holders in my bathroom.

It was MaKhumalo, speaking isiNdebele, a language common to the south of the country, who told me about previous inmates of the prison. One of the cells on the floor below us, she said, had been occupied at one point by Simon Mann, an English mercenary who had been detained in Zimbabwe before being extradited to Equatorial Guinea, where he was given a 34-year prison sentence for his role in a failed coup d'état in 2004. In 2009 he received a presidential pardon and was freed. Another occupant of a cell on that floor was Masendeke, a notorious robber.

We learned from the lawyers that the men, including Broderick, who had been held at Harare Central prison since Christmas Eve, had been moved to Chikurubi. The cholera outbreak, compounded by the acute shortage of clean water, was also taking its toll at Chikurubi. The shortage of food was another serious problem – scores of inmates developed pellagra and a significant number died either of starvation or cholera.

It was normal to pass by dozens of dead bodies every day, especially in the morning in the reception area on my way to the visitors' booth. Some inmates could no longer walk and were carried by fellow inmates to the hospital or to the visitors' booth. The situation was tough for most Zimbabweans during this time and most visitors brought very little for the inmates.

Most of the male inmates only received one meal a day – *sadza*, with no salt, or boiled vegetables with no oil. The *sadza*, which is ordinarily white, was usually brown indicating that the maize was rotten, full of weevils and not fit for human consumption. It had also been badly ground – whole kernels of maize were visible.

I was in prison at the same time as Godfrey Nzira, also known as 'Madzibaba Nzira', who was serving a sentence for raping women in his congregation. Prison officers, both male and female, visited his cell regularly for some 'holy anointing' and, in return, he received special treatment. Busloads of congregants, all clad in white garments, would come to be anointed. He would be controversially pardoned by President Mugabe on medical grounds in 2011. His welcome home party was attended by senior government and Zanu-PF officials. He died later that year.

Visiting times gave me an opportunity to see Broderick and Pascal. Our families arranged to come together so that we could also see each other. On one visit I met *sekuru* Chiramba and was shocked at his appearance. His blood pressure was so high his face was swollen and it was three days before anything was done about it.

Pascal was released in mid-January and arrangements were made for Nigel to be taken to his maternal grandmother. The environment was becoming unbearable for him – he did not take well to being locked up for the night at any time between 15h30 and 16h00 and, in addition, the prison, like all other parts of the country, experienced power cuts and, surrounded by cold, high walls in a dark cell Nigel cried uncontrollably. At one point a compassionate officer searched for a rechargeable light to console him.

Three white men had joined the inmates at Chikurubi. They were incarcerated for allegedly training youths on their farms.

Takudzwa turned 18 while I was in prison and on his birthday I sang for him from behind the bars in the visitors' booth. I also learned that my priest, Reverend Cleopas Marandu, and Reverend Sam Sifelani, a family friend from Gweru, had tried to get permission to give me Holy Communion but the authorities had blocked them. For Anglicans, receiving Holy Communion in a difficult situation is comforting.

The inmates from Banket and Chinhoyi – Concilia, Violet, Pieta and Audrey – did not have as many visitors as I did because of the distance and the appalling economic situation. This meant that those who were married were only able to see their spouses when we went to court. We approached the prison social worker for help and she facilitated regular visits between the spouses.

Several times Chief Superintendent Magwenzi tried to sign out inmates without the knowledge of the lawyers and in all instances he failed. One day the officer in charge summoned us to his office to solve the deadlock and asked Magwenzi to call Beatrice, whose contact number I had memorised. Beatrice asked Magwenzi to put the call on speakerphone. He informed her that by refusing to allow us to go to police headquarters for what he termed 'clarifications' she was jeopardising our chances of being granted bail.

In response we heard Beatrice ask him how many court orders the police had failed to comply with and tell him firmly that she would not have her clients harassed.

Chief Superintendent Magwenzi and Beatrice eventually came to an agreement wherein Magwenzi would sign out Concilia and Violet and Beatrice would join them at Magwenzi's office. On one of his daily visits Cosmas spotted Magwenzi coming in. Worried that I might disappear again, he advised me not to agree to be signed out by Magwenzi without

77

the knowledge of the lawyers.

I received books from many people and initially my family tried to bring me daily newspapers, but, because my case was receiving considerable publicity, by the time the prison censors had removed all articles that mentioned my name, what remained were strips of paper. The only complete pages were the classified and sports sections. I withdrew my request for daily newspapers.

Until I saw the newspapers then I had no idea that my disappearance and now the court appearances had been covered so widely in all the newspapers in Zimbabwe apart from those that were state owned. I recalled that one day Cosmas, the operative, had come into my room holding the *Financial Gazette*, known as the 'pink paper'. '*Sisi* I wish I could give you this paper to read but unfortunately I can't,' he had said. I later realised the article he was pointing to must have been about me.

At the second interrogation centre the heavily built man had blurted out, apparently out of the blue, 'It seems your organisation is not just known in Zimbabwe but is well known throughout the world.' At the time I had not understood what he was alluding to, now it began to make sense, as did the attention I seemed to attract every time I was moved to a new place.

During my incarceration I interacted with many people who should not have been in prison at all. One of them was Nyasha, who also had a child with her. She was one of the inmates from the female section who brought water and food to the Maximum Security prison, Nyasha's jovial nature disguised the pain she lived with.

Nyasha was serving a 27-year jail term for stock theft because of the cruelty of her husband's uncle, MaKhumalo told me. Stock theft is a serious offence in Zimbabwe – conviction for the theft of one cow results in a nine-year prison sentence. Nyasha had been a caretaker at the uncle's homestead when three head of cattle went missing. Neighbours had told the uncle that Nyasha had sold them. She was arrested, tried in Mutare, and sentenced. According to a prison official, who knew the family well, all the cows had subsequently been recovered but Nyasha was not released.

Nyasha received no visits, not even from her husband or her family, as a result of a cultural practice whereby a family disowns a loved one not because they do not love the person but as a protest against the person's ill treatment. Nyasha's family believed they could not visit her in prison because the Nyasha they knew was not in prison – thus they punished her instead of the husband's family, who, once the cows had been recovered, should have facilitated the release of mother and child.

Determined to try to help Nyasha, I told her story to two lawyer colleagues after I was released but even to this day I have not received any news about her.

MaKhumalo applied unsuccessfully several times for presidential amnesty, although, when the new Constitution came into effect on 22 May 2013, abolishing the death penalty for women, she no longer faced execution. Her children visited her regularly on public holidays and made sure that she was provided with food. She had taken her case to the Constitutional Court to ensure that the provision was respected but, sadly, before she learned of her fate, she fell ill and died on 15 July 2014. It broke my heart that I had been unable to see her before she died – the last time I had tried to visit the guards had refused to allow me in.

My lawyers filed two applications on my behalf, which Judge Alphas Chitakunye heard in his chambers. The first was for the police to name the people who had handed me to them, particularly in view of the fact that the same police, through their chief legal advisor, assistant Commissioner Nzombe, in a letter to the lawyers had indicated that my disappearance was being treated as a kidnapping and that the perpetrators would be brought to book.

The Minister of State Security, Didymus Mutasa, who filed a responding affidavit, opposed the application, confirming that my abduction and detention in the hands of state security agents was sanctioned by the state. He also contended that the state security agents should not be identified since the investigations were ongoing.

In the second application the lawyers sought an order for me to be taken for urgent medical examination and treatment based on the affidavits lodged by the doctors who had examined us at Chikurubi prison. The ruling on the two applications was delivered on 2 January 2009.

Judge Chitakunye accepted the affidavit lodged by Minister Mutasa and refused to order the identification of the agents or their prosecution but he did order that I be examined at the Avenues Clinic.

After consulting the deputy commissioner of prisons, my lawyers hit a brick wall in their efforts to have me moved to Avenues Clinic when Mrs Chifodya, the officer in charge of Chikurubi female prison, after consulting the deputy commissioner of prisons, defied the court order.

An urgent application was filed for all 18 abductees to be examined at the clinic on the strength of the doctors' affidavits, but, although urgent, the application was not heard quickly – it seemed as though various judges avoided it like the plague.

| Another Step Towards Freedom

' E vidence gathered proves that she is a threat to society and she should not be released now.' These were the words of Johannes Tomana, the Attorney General, in an interview with the *Herald* in January 2009. The evidence was, of course, a false confession extracted through torture.

It was16 January 2009 and I was back in the dock. MaKhumalo had put knife pleats into my green dress so I would look immaculate for my appearance. On that day I walked in without leg irons or handcuffs as these had been removed before we left the red van, which now drove into the underground cells to avoid the media taking pictures of us in prison garb.

Magistrate Archie Wochiunga had the unenviable task of delivering a ruling in an application for my case to be referred to the Constitutional Court. The intention was to challenge my continued prosecution in light of the numerous violations of my pre-trial rights that I had endured. I emphasised that my right to personal liberty, right to protection against inhumane and degrading treatment and right to the protection of the law were violated during the time I was disappeared.

Magistrate Wochiunga took his position and wasted no time. 'Will the accused stand,' he commanded, before reading his ruling.

'This court rules in favour of the accused. The application before me is neither frivolous nor vexatious,' he said, as the prosecution and defence team bowed to acknowledge the ruling. At that stage, not fully appreciating that this was my gateway to freedom, I saw it only as a small victory, though worth celebrating.

I spent only a brief time in court – it seems that Magistrate Wochiunga did not realise that when proceedings were dragged out they afforded me an opportunity to spend time with family, even at a distance. As the court took a break Takudzwa, who was in the company of his uncles and Vincent, signalled victory by crossing his hand across his chest and beamed at me. I took it to mean 'hang in there, the process is starting to show a glimmer of hope'.

When the same application had been taken to the Supreme Court prior to this, Chief Justice Godfrey Chidyausiku had launched a scathing attack on the defence team for bringing a defective application, which, according to the Constitution, should have been directed to the Magistrate's Court. The *Herald* crowed 'dismissed', failing to note that the dismissal was based on a mere procedural error. Now it was my chance to crow and I laughed last and loudest.

My fellow inmates were overjoyed when I told them the news. The hopes of the 'lawyers and judges' behind bars – both prison officers and inmates are uncelebrated 'learned colleagues' – were raised too as they discussed the law of precedence.

Broderick's and Audrey's applications for referral to the Constitutional Court were due to be heard the next day. Celebrations were in order and we sang gospel songs across the high walls.

CHAPTER
ten | Still Only A Number

O n 20 January, the day that the first African American president, Barack Obama, was inaugurated, two senior female officers and three armed male officers accompanied me to the Avenues Clinic. A few days earlier, Chief Justice Godfrey Chidyausiku, sitting in chambers, had ordered that I be examined urgently. Although the order appeared to be complied with there was only a semblance of compliance.

As usual I was a spectacle as I arrived at the clinic, where most staff and patients were packed in the reception area glued to television sets showing Obama's inauguration. They were also keen to catch a glimpse of Jestina Mukoko, the now notorious former news anchor who had committed the very serious offence of recruiting a single police officer to overthrow the government.

Dr Douglas Gwatidzo, who, at the time, was the chairperson of the Zimbabwe Doctors for Human Rights, examined me. One of the female prison officers initially ignored Dr Gwatidzo's request for doctor-client confidentiality. 'These are concrete walls and this room has no windows. If you want more reinforcements outside get them, but I need to attend to Jestina alone,' he said. After several requests the officer slowly opened the door, walked out and closed it again behind her.

Although I had never met Dr Gwatidzo before, this was the first time since 3 December that I had felt safe, and tears pierced my eyes. The officer, and perhaps several others,were just outside the door but for that moment I could make Dr Gwatidzo understand my pain and how I had been bruised.

Dr Gwatidzo took time to console me. 'Jestina,' he said, 'we have all been worried about you. 'He excused himself briefly to call a fellow human rights activist and friend, Primrose Matambanadzo, the Director of Zimbabwe Doctors for Human Rights, to tell her I was there.

'In the past it would have been very difficult for us to detect symptoms consistent with the torture that you describe, but not anymore,' Dr Gwatidzo told me. Concerned about my high blood pressure and high blood sugar, he ordered an intravenous drip and I was wheeled off to have my legs scanned and my chest X-rayed. I did not get the name of the doctor who performed the scan, but, on setting her eyes on the shackled figure on the bed she turned to the guard. 'I don't think I can attend to her chained up like that.'

'But...I am not supposed to remove ...' stammered the guard. 'If that is the case then I am not going to waste my time in here, I have other patients waiting,' said the doctor, starting to remove her gloves. The guard jumped up, took out her keys and did the honourable thing. I always think of this unsung human rights defender who, unknowingly, was putting her life in danger by boldly demanding that her health ethics be respected.

The examinations at the hospital confirmed that I needed urgent treatment for the high blood pressure and blood sugar and the scan confirmed dilated veins, which are consistent with the soles of the feet being beaten. The prison officers got busy on their mobile phones consulting someone from their head office, referred to only as Gaka, who told them that there was no way I could be admitted to this hospital. When your identity is reduced to a number you lose control over your own life, it is those in control who determine what is going to happen when and how, regardless of the impact of the decision on your survival or your right to life.

While Dr Gwatidzo tried to reason with the officers Gaka charged into the clinic like a whirlwind, shouting at the top of his voice, 'Take her back to Chikurubi now!! There is a car waiting outside.' There was no time to remove the drip and back in handcuffs and leg irons, I struggled to balance it in my hands.

When I was back in my cell a nurse from the prison hospital was summoned to hang up the drip. The next morning a team from the prison hospital was concerned about both the high blood pressure and the high blood sugar. I had never been hypertensive and, although there is a history of diabetes in my family – both Cosmas and Peter are diabetic – I had never had a problem before. By early morning the drip was finished and it began to draw blood from the vein it was connected to and became painful. MaKhumalo helped me to bath. My mother was worried about my health when she visited later that day. She did not understand why I had not been admitted to hospital the previous day.

Dr Makanza, the Chikurubi prison doctor, was not in attendance and a Dr Dhobbie, from Harare Central Prison, came to remove the drip well after 15h00. Later that afternoon a senior female prison officer, one of the two who had accompanied me to the Avenues Clinic, came into the prison yard panting – for a woman her size walking up two flights of stairs was not child's play.

She informed me that I was to be admitted to the prison hospital. Turning to the officer on duty she instructed her to put on the leg irons and handcuffs that were standard when maximum security prisoners crossed the prison courtyard.

Walking in leg irons and handcuffs is an art and practice makes it easier. The steps have to be small and dainty. Leg irons hurt the ankles and although I wore thick football socks, which had been brought to me from home, if a step was not in sync there was a pinch. As I crossed the prison courtyard on the way to the hospital, shackled and tackling each step with caution, the senior officer accompanying me remarked unpleasantly: 'Jestina, you are quite good at walking in leg irons.'

She made it sound as though I was a habitual class D prisoner. I fumed, but could say nothing. The other officers laughed as though it was some kind of joke. The senior officer was the one who, on our first day in maximum security, had wanted to keep us confined apart from 30 minutes a day in the courtyard.

On one occasion, when she had accompanied me to the visitors' booth she had paraded me for close to 25 minutes, making me stand against a wall on the other side of the bars while my family was on the other side not knowing what was happening until a fellow male officer enquired, 'Officer is there a problem, you have been standing there for a while? The booth is getting crowded.' She mumbled something inaudible and signalled for me to move forward to speak to my now anxious visitors.

Before my eventual admission to Avenues Clinic she was the officer who had tried to force me and two other inmates to go for examination at the ill-equipped prison hospital. Just before I left Chikurubi, news of new promotions filtered in – this officer, together with her husband, were among those who had been promoted.

The hospital was only intended for male inmates and the office of the officer in charge had to be converted into a hospital ward for me. I was greeted by a multitude of prison officers of all ranks who were milling around the ward ready to take up their duty of looking after this dangerous criminal.

A bed had been prepared (for me) on the floor, the most senior officer had a real bed. Throughout the night my blood pressure and blood sugar were monitored every two hours. The hospital environment was unsettling and there was a stench that made me uneasy. As soon as my levels showed slight signs of improvement the next day I requested to be returned to my cell.

On 12 February the officer in charge of Chikurubi maximum security summoned me to announce my second visit to the Avenues Clinic. *Sekuru* Chiramba and Gandhi Mudzingwa were the other inmates in the red van with me. We had refused to be examined at the prison hospital and the over-zealous female officer tried to make us sign something, but we refused.

Chief Superintendent Magwenzi was also waiting in his car but the support unit escort vehicles were nowhere to be seen. We waited briefly and Magwenzi, who clearly had delusions of grandeur and wanted us to believe he was more important than he was, suggested passing through the support unit headquarters to get an escort. The lawyers, who were waiting at the gate, followed us to the support unit, where Magwenzi was embarrassed by the fact that the security guards would not allow him to override their procedures, so we proceeded without a vehicle to escort us.

At the clinic, Dr Gwatidzo examined us individually in the company of the prison doctor, Makanza, and both confirmed that I needed to be admitted urgently. Again the prison officers disputed this and, as had happened the first time, they prepared to take me back to Chikurubi. This time, though, the staff at the clinic breathed fire, demanding that if the officers insisted on taking us back to prison they sign a document to confirm that they had acted against the advice of the hospital. One of the prison officers signed the papers, but I am not sure whether he understood the implications of what he was doing.

When we arrived back, we found that a joyous mood had engulfed the entire prison facility. The usually dreary and melancholy atmosphere was replaced by loud laughter and conversation as each officer tried to be heard over the others. 'I saluted him several times until he told me to stop,' said one of the officers at reception, demonstrating the scene.

While we had been away the newly sworn in Prime Minister and his delegation had visited the prison to see the abductees-turned-inmates. As the gates to the cells opened Audrey shouted that Tsvangirai had particularly asked after me.

Well after 11 that night, when all the excitement had died down, the phone rang and the officer on duty announced, 'Jestina, the officer in charge wants to see you in his office. Someone is coming up to open for you.' The officer in charge told me that an ambulance was on the way to take me to be admitted to hospital.

After the two previous unsuccessful attempts to have me admitted I did not hide my disbelief, but he said, with unusual courtesy, 'Miss Mukoko, things are about to change. Trust me.' This was the second time that I was being told that things were about to change. First it was by Cosmas at the detention centre and now it was the officer in charge of Chikurubi.

The journey to the hospital took a long time – the ambulance, which had no headlights, moved at a snail's pace. Accompanying me in the ambulance were *sekuru* Chiramba and Gandhi Mudzingwa, who kept me laughing as we recalled how Magwenzi had been embarrassed earlier at the Support Unit.

At the hospital the three of us were admitted to the same ward in the High Dependency Unit. For the first time in weeks I was able to discard the green uniform and, as I took it off, I prayed softly that I would never have to put it on again. In fact I would do so, but for less than 24 hours, when I was committed to Chikurubi in May before I was indicted in the High Court.

The nurse on duty insisted that I take a bath before slipping into the clean night clothes laid out on the bed. 'I think you will sleep better if you bath, the water is hot,' she said. I was not keen to bath, I felt so tired after the shuttling to and fro in the afternoon and the slow ambulance, but I eventually gave in when I recognised that the nurse might be worried about the hospital linen being infested with the lice.

In fact, the blankets we had used in the cells in Chikurubi, and the environment, were clean, it was our male colleagues who complained of blankets and clothes infested with lice. I did feel better after the bath, though I was embarrassed by the presence of a female prison officer watching me and refusing to move for fear that I might escape. This was the only time a prison officer deprived me of privacy while I was in hospital. All the others sat outside and kept watch at the door.

After so many weeks away from home I slipped into crisply ironed white sheets on a real bed. *Gogo* Dizha sent a word of caution when she heard about my admission. 'Tell her to be careful, she might fall off the bed she has not slept in a bed in a while.' Although I was no longer wearing handcuffs, I was still shackled by leg irons fixed to one leg and attached to the bed post. The nurse on duty protested, but she lost the battle. It was difficult to rest fully – my blood pressure and blood sugar were monitored every two hours and the leg irons were uncomfortable. At six in the morning I took another bath.

The doctor who arrived in the morning was ready to fight, demanding that my legs, which, because of the hours of torture were the greatest source of my pain, be set free. He, too, lost the battle but later, during the course of my stay, the guards left the leg irons on the bed post but did not shackle me, asking me to hold the leg irons down so that they would not get into trouble with their superiors. One of the senior officers would always remark, 'leg irons are only removed from an inmate in hospital when they are wheeled to the mortuary'.

When the news of my admission spread, even those who had feared being seen at Chikurubi came to visit. Because of the large numbers of visitors each was only given a few minutes and I was allowed only two visitors at any given time. All visitors were screened before being allowed in. Cosmas had to visit Harare Central Prison regularly to have the list of visitors renewed, complete with identity numbers and addresses. None of them, however, was a member of the diplomatic corps – the Ministry of Foreign Affairs had forbidden diplomats from visiting.

The ward became a hive of activity, with an army of prison officers both inside the ward and at the door and numerous visitors for the three of us. Gandhi's and *sekuru* Chiramba's beds were close to each other, with mine opposite, and the open space between my bed and the windows became a camping site for the officers inside the ward.

Two days after my admission I had a special visitor. Dr Sanyanga's mother had arrived from Gweru. An exception to the two-visitor rule was made for her and she was allowed to sit through all visits. On that first day she had barely sat down when she started making changes. The first was to the hairstyle I had been wearing since November. She managed to get permission to bring in a pair of scissors to undo the hairstyle and trim my hair. The prison officers had no problems with that, they were the most understanding group with whom I had interacted during my stay in prison. Most of them were not from Chikurubi but from Harare Central Prison.

One of my most illustrious visitors was Prime Minister Morgan Tsvangirai. His arrival, with a delegation that included Deputy Prime Minister Thokozani Khuphe and Nelson Chamisa, then Minister of Information, Communication, and Technology, caused much excitement among the officers on duty. I had learned earlier that Deputy Prime Minister Khuphe's mother had been admitted in the ward next to mine.

I told the Prime Minister about the absurd accusation that I had been recruiting for his party. 'This is ending very soon and I am sorry you had to go through this experience. We are not going to rest until all of you are granted bail as soon as possible,' he said.

There had been a prolonged delay between the signing of the Global Political Agreement and the consummation of the coalition government and it is believed that Tsvangirai had been shown the video clips that were recorded at the second interrogation centre and in Magwenzi's office as a way of putting pressure on him to agree to establish the coalition government. That is why my brother Cosmas believed I was a pawn in a larger political game.

Believing that in order to have me freed he should approach Tsvangirai, who had broken his earlier promise not to be sworn in until all the abductees had been released, Cosmas tried to approach the new Prime Minister at a celebration after the swearing in. He was hoping to hear from Tsvangirai himself whether the matter of the abductees had been discussed and what was the decision. However, he never reached Tsvangirai – the guards at the gate had prevented him from going in.

Tsvangirai's visit was the subject of discussion among the prison officers for much of the evening, with some approaching me to put in a good word for them. What they did not know was that before the abduction Prime Minister Tsvangirai would have had no reason to visit me as he did not know me personally. The next day I had a visit from his wife, Susan, who was to die in a car crash only a few days later.

One night, as new officers were taking over guard duty, one came in in an unusually jovial mood, shouting at the top of her voice, 'I can now afford to buy bread. Not just bread, but margarine as well. The United States dollar is powerful.' She waved her loaf of bread for all to see and as soon as she arrived, she made tea, something she had not done in a very long time.

The officer was referring to the fact that the Zimbabwe dollar was making way for a multi-currency economy. The skyrocketing inflation rate of the past years had meant that the rate of the Zimbabwe dollar against the US dollar changed several times in a single day, making it useless by the time the money reached the bank accounts of many government employees. Now, with their salaries pegged in US dollars, the currency would stabilise and they could, at last, afford to buy bread and would no longer have to survive on homemade bread that lacked many ingredients. They could also pay for transport to and from work.

A few days after the visit of the Prime Minister information began to filter in of warrants of liberation issued for some of my fellow inmates. Broderick was granted bail, but, at the same time, he lost his father, so, instead of his family celebrating his freedom they were confronted with a bereavement. Broderick visited me before he travelled to his rural home for the burial of his father. Sekuru Chiramba, who was also released, continued to remain in hospital and receive treatment, but as a free man. Concilia, Emmanuel, Pieta, Audrey, Violet and Collen were also freed.

Before the releases took place, the state, through Florence Ziyambi, continued to insist that I should be back at Chikurubi. In an effort to establish whether I was in a condition to go back to prison Magistrate Gloria Takundwa held a brief court session in the hospital ward. The magistrate ruled that the court was satisfied that I was not well and needed to be in the care of the Avenues Clinic, which was fully equipped to deal with my symptoms.

I was to remain in hospital for a further week, after which my condition would be further assessed. On 2 March Beatrice informed me that she had been called to the Attorney General's office and told that I would be granted bail if I withdrew the court challenge. She assured me that such an agreement was not enforceable in law.

The bail conditions were stringent. I had to deposit US$600 and provide surety of an immovable property worth US$20 000 in the form of a title deed. I also had to surrender my travel document and report to the police at Norton police station every Monday and Friday between 6h00 and 18h00. I remained in hospital until 6 March.

My discharge from the hospital and return to the home I had been removed from a little more than three months before caused huge excitement. My sisters-in-law Patricia and Alice, who had not seen me during my detention, had just arrived from Gweru. While I tried to catch up with visitors and took time to open each and every letter of solidarity, sent mainly by supporters of Amnesty International, the news broke of the fatal accident that claimed the life of Susan Tsvangirai and injured the Prime Minister.

I decided to travel with *gogo* Dizha to Seke communal lands for a breath of fresh air and to get away from everything. My late husband is buried on a small anthill on his parents' homestead. This gave me the opportunity also to visit my husband's paternal grandmother, *gogo* Sylvia, who, more than 100 years old, was ill and in her last days.

When I was in Chikurubi *gogo* Sylvia, a devout Anglican, had sent me several messages reminding me to read the Holy Bible and to remember that she would not die in my absence as, if she did, there would be no one to take photographs of her coffin.

A visionary woman in her own right, she was concerned that my activities might rip her family apart. She was aware that my work as a human rights activist was not appreciated by those in Zanu-PF, the party her son, my father-in-law, belongs to. In my conversations with her, *gogo* Sylvia told me of her concerns. 'I have asked your father-in law-but with no satisfactory answer about what he would do if you were the target of guns from his side.' *Gogo* Sylvia died peacefully in May 2009.

I was really frightened about having to report to the police. After my experiences I was terrified that I would walk into the police station and be told that there was an order for them to hold me. I never went unaccompanied by someone I trusted, usually a family member. On one occasion, May Day, my companion was human rights lawyer Alec Muchadehama.

Early that morning the intercom at home had buzzed several times, waking everybody in the house. The dogs were barking outside but when Vincent eventually answered there was no response from the other side. My brother Simon and his wife, who were alerted, took a walk past the house but did not see anyone. The lawyers were informed and it was decided that Alec should accompany me to the police station.

On 4 May I was served with an indictment issued by the Attorney General's office to appear in court on charges of terrorism and sabotage. All the other abductees were charged with the same offences. In terms of section 66(1) of the Criminal Procedure and Evidence Act, I had to be committed to prison and go through the process of applying for bail again. The defence team opposed the revocation of bail, arguing that bail had not been granted by any court, it had been the result of a political intervention and thus could not be cancelled by a court.

Magistrate Catherine Chimwanda, who presided over the hearing, postponed the matter to the following day to allow her to consult. On 5 May she ruled that she did not have the jurisdiction to consider the issue of bail and therefore I was committed again to Chikurubi Maximum Security prison. I received my warrant of liberation less than 24 hours later and, on 6 May, I was free again.

Initially, the conditions were stringent. I had to report every Monday and every Friday. It was challenging to organise a trip away from Norton and still adhere to the conditions. If I had to travel over a weekend it had to be after reporting on a Friday and I had to ensure that I was close to Norton police station by Monday between 6h00 and 18h00.

The next big thing that I dealt with was the fear of continuing to live in the house in Norton. In the months that I was out on bail I found it difficult to sleep, imagining that the abductors were at the gate. Friends and relatives tried to help me, suggesting that if I woke up in fear I should go to the gate to satisfy myself that there was nobody there. I never tried this as it would have felt like walking into the clutches of a hunting lion.

The best thing for me was to move into a new environment, in Harare, where lawyers would be able to respond quickly if anything happened to me. For a few days I was able to sleep in the new place but in no time, in the same way as anaesthetic wears off, I began to experience sleeping problems again. If I took a sleeping tablet it stopped being effective hours before it was time to wake up. I was easily irritable and I cringed at a knock on the door or just the turning of a key.

On one occasion I shouted at Takudzwa for forgetting to lock the doors, something I bitterly regretted when he opened up to me later about how the situation was tearing him apart. His worst fear was losing me. After going through weeks of therapy and taking medication for post-traumatic stress disorder for six months, Takudzwa could not hide his joy when I finally returned to my old self.

After staying with me for a few weeks my mother announced that she was going back to Gweru. I travelled with her after I had completed the reporting rituals and recognised that a lot of people in Gweru were not at ease around me. My sister-in-law Patricia, Tofara's mother, who lives close to my mother and keeps an eye on her house whenever she is away, acknowledged that 'there are people around us who wished the worst but there are others who have been genuinely praying for your safe return'.

CHAPTER
eleven | The State Is Challenged

The constitutional challenge, in which I applied for a stay of criminal prosecution on the grounds that the way I had been treated contaminated the entire legal process, was heard on 25 June 2009 in the Supreme Court, sitting on that day as the Constitutional Court. Fatima Maxwell, a lawyer with the Attorney General's office, appeared for the state and Advocate Jeremy Gauntlett, who lives and works in Cape Town, led the defence team.

As I disembarked from the car a flurry of photographers clicked away. I was accompanied by a smaller contingent of the family. Cosmas had arrived early the same day from Gweru. Initially he was not keen to come, but Vincent convinced him, saying that this might be the most important of the court appearances he had attended. My youngest brother, Simon, was also with me, as was Vincent.

Although the family team was smaller, the Supreme Court was packed to capacity and there was hardly space for us to sit. Civil society colleagues made way for the other members of the family while I found a place between Dzimbabwe Chimbga and Irene Petras, two friends from the Zimbabwe Lawyers for Human Rights.

Among those gathered just outside the courtroom were civil society colleagues, diplomats, politicians, journalists, the team from the Attorney General's office and human rights lawyers. There was an observer from the Southern African Litigation Centre. This was the first time I had been in the Supreme Court and I was not sure what to expect.

Compared to the Magistrate's Court this one was clean and showed no signs of the extensive disrepair evident in the lower court. I had been told that it might take a long time before the ruling was handed down – it sometimes takes two or more years.

The courtroom pulsated with conversation and I felt as though I was the only person in a lonely world as I drowned in my thoughts. Although I was no longer in the green dress, nor was I in handcuffs or leg irons, somehow I still felt restrained.

The noise and my thoughts were interrupted when the judges made their way into the court. They were Chief Justice Godfrey Chidyausiku and Justices Luke Malaba, Vernanda Ziyambi, Wilson Sandura and Paddington Garwe. Their attire –white wigs and red robes – emphasised the formality of the process.

'Is it normal that a citizen is arrested in this way?' enquired the Chief Justice.

'No, my Lord,' replied Fatima Maxwell.

'In your experience as a lawyer and what is provided for in the Constitution would you say this is the way it should be done?' he asked.

'No, my Lord', Maxwell responded.

'Would it be correct to say the rights of the applicant were violated?' asked Justice Malaba

'Yes, my Lord,' replied Fatima Maxwell.

This was the first time Fatima Maxwell had represented the state officials had named in my court application, up to now the star prosecutor had been Florence Ziyambi. Fatima was not prepared for this appearance. At one point her papers scattered and dotted the floor as she stuttered to respond to the questions being fired from the bench.

She appeared uncertain of some of the facts, for instance, whether my head was on the seat of the car or on somebody's lap. 'The applicant was on the witness stand and that is where you should have asked her that question,' was the Chief Justice's response.

When she expressed doubts about whether I had been tortured by my captors, who remained nameless, the court advised her that it had been in her power to get testimonies from the state agents without identifying them. When she said she had not been involved in this case until then, she was told that once she knew she would be appearing it was up to her to make an effort to prepare for the process.

Advocate Gauntlett took me back to 3 December as he described to the court how my rights were violated. As I retraced, with him, my steps from that day, my body demanded to release the screams and tears that were eating away at it, both emotionally and physically.

'The process [of my arrest] is so contaminated that you should order a stay of prosecution,' stated Advocate Gauntlett, highlighting the extent to which state security agents colluded with the police to violate my rights in contravention of the Constitution. He listed nine points that he believed should guide the court in its decision.

- no warrant of arrest
- subjection to inhuman and degrading treatment
- unlawful detention
- solitary confinement
- torture
- threats of harm
- deprivation of medical care
- deprivation of access to a lawyer
- connivance between the police and state security agents

As Gauntlett addressed the court I was in my own world. I could almost touch some of my tormentors and their threats echoed in my ears. 'You have a choice of becoming a state witness or going extinct. We can bury you around here and no one will ever know.'

The Chief Justice reserved judgement and, as I walked out of the court I heard someone comment: 'From what transpired today I do not see this court ruling in any other way but with these courts you can never be certain...' Before I left the building a doctor friend approached me. 'I think you need to speak to someone. I was watching you throughout the court proceedings. I am sending someone to your office.'

Since my days in hospital I had had regular counselling sessions and for a few weeks I thought I was on the mend, only to realise that I was still a bundle of nerves. The sessions with counsellors helped me to unwind and pour my heart out. Unlike my family, the counsellors helped to encourage the tears that were tearing me up inside by not stopping my outpouring of emotions. My family, on the other hand, would try to console me, not wanting to see me cry. What they were not aware of is that the pain and the tears if left inside would gnaw away at me. My doctor friend sent a counsellor and we had a number of sessions, spanning a few weeks.

While we were waiting for the judgement I was summoned to Takudzwa's school. There had been a case of impropriety – a girl had scaled the perimeter wall and had been found in Takudzwa's room. With all the publicity over my abduction and trial, Takudzwa, already popular, had become something of a celebrity, especially with the girls. The letter that summoned me informed me that the girl's parents would be there too, but when Cosmas and I arrived there was no sign of them and we were left waiting for several hours before being attended to. The school suspended Takudzwa briefly and I could not help feeling that the way they had handled the matter was somehow related to my ongoing ordeal.

On 25 September Harrison Nkomo called me and dropped a bombshell. 'The court is handing down judgement on Monday 28 September.' I had thought I still had a long time to wait and this was at the stroke of three months. I received the call when I was in the car with Vincent, who had become my personal driver since I had returned home. Still in fear that would be abducted again, I had not yet summoned up the courage to be on my own or to drive myself.

At the time, I was making last-minute preparations to travel to Mhondoro communal lands 110 km from Harare for a memorial service for my mother's late sister. I told Vincent what the call was about and he sensed my uneasiness. 'From what happened that day in court I don't see why you should be worried,' he reassured me. What else could he say? But I was worried – why was this judgement going to be delivered in record time.

I began to call the other family members, many of whom were already on their way to Mhondoro. My mother's late sister, her last surviving biological sibling, was a woman with whom the entire family had shared a bond. She was a forthright, fearless woman, who did not hesitate to call a spade a spade. Despite my nervousness about the judgement there was no way I could stay away from the Mhondoro event. As we drove there we speculated about it and, when we met the other members of the family, there was more speculation and they all tried to comfort me.

On a sunny September day the Supreme Court building was bustling with activity – even more than it had been for the original hearing. The courtroom was jam-packed and some people had to be content with being in an overflow room. The three judges took their place and Chief Justice Godfrey Chidyausiku wasted no time in handing down a unanimous judgement: 'The state, through its agents, violated the applicant's constitutional rights to the extent of entitling the applicant a permanent stay of criminal prosecution.'

I was in a brief daze, not sure whether I had heard correctly. The people next to me reached out for congratulatory hugs as Harrison walked over to shake my hand and Cosmas, who was mobbed, wore a broad smile. He was not the only one smiling, the room was engulfed by a jovial atmosphere. I was not sure my legs would be able to carry me once all the hugging stopped. The noise in the courtroom was deafening as people wove through the crowds to reach where I sat, still bewildered.

As more people reached out and reality sank in, my eyes flooded. I was not sure whether they were tears of joy but I was reminded of the extreme pain I had endured, in particular in the 21 days at the secret detention centre when everyone outside thought I was dead. My sister-in-law, Sibongile, rushed to hold my hand and I took time to talk to the group of people gathered outside the courtroom.

Beatrice was not in court when the judgment was handed down but Harrison called her as soon as we stepped out of court. He rushed towards me, mobile phone in hand. 'Jestina,' said Beatrice, 'I am sorry I was not there with you but I am so happy for you. Now you can get on with a normal life.' She also advised me that I should retrieve my impounded passport and get back my bail deposit. The latter took two visits from Harrison to the clerk of court.

Speaking briefly to journalists for the first time I could not hold back the emotions that choked me when I tried to express how painful it was to learn that people could act the way my tormentors had, knowing full well that they were breaking the law and violating the rights of an innocent citizen. There are times in life when the world just continues to collapse.

When the media approached Fatima Maxwell as she left the court her response was a curt 'No comment'. As far as I know, the state made no official statement either. The full judgement only became available in October 2012, more than three years after it was handed down.

In a 41-page document the Constitutional Court explained how it had reached its decision. Among its statements was the following:

No exceptional circumstance such as the seriousness of the crime the person is suspected of having committed, or the danger he or she is believed to pose to national security can justify infliction of torture, or inhuman or degrading treatment. There cannot be a value in our society over which there is so clear a consensus as the prohibition of torture inhuman and degrading treatment of a person in the custody of a public official. That such a treatment should never form part of the techniques of investigation of crimes employed by law enforcement agents, is a restatement of the principle that the law which it is their duty to enforce, requires that only fair and humane treatment ought to be applied to a person under criminal investigation.

Forcing the applicant to kneel for a long time on mounds of

gravel whilst being interrogated, falls within the meaning of torture. The treatment to which she was subjected was premeditated. The severe pain and suffering she was forced to endure was intentionally inflicted.

When I saw more relatives outside the court I wailed uncontrollably. The ruling and the full judgement revealed the callousness of state agents. While they inflicted wounds on my feet which I have had to live with all these years what is most painful is the fact that I had not been treated like a human being.

CHAPTER
twelve | Back In The World

For several days after the judgement I was in the news. 'Jestina Mukoko is acquitted', 'Mukoko acquittal lays bare state terrorism', and 'Zimbabwe drops activist charges'. However, while the private media, both local and international, tried to cover this development the state media tried to pretend that nothing had happened.

It was not easy to get used to being a free citizen again. It was as though my life had stopped on 3 December 2008 and I only reclaimed it nine months later. I no longer had to report to the police. On the first Friday after the ruling I was anxious. I had a nagging feeling the whole day that I had overlooked doing something very important.

When I drove around Harare I made it my business to peep into suspicious looking vehicles searching for blindfolds. I also kept my eyes open for the faces I had seen during my internment but saw none of them, apart from the assistant commissioner I met at Harare International Airport. Even as

I religiously looked out for suspicious vehicles and tried to identify my tormentors I had no idea what I would do if I saw any of them.

With my passport back I travelled to several parts of the world. First I went to the USA, where I was invited to present a paper at Syracuse University and was honoured to meet the then US Secretary of State Hillary Clinton, and the First Lady, Michelle Obama. I also travelled to Ireland, where I met the teams that had campaigned for my release and I attended mass with the congregation in Belfast that had dedicated prayers for me.

To celebrate International Human Rights Day in 2009 the City of Weimer in Germany handed me the Human Rights Prize and, while I was away the National Association of Non-Governmental Organisations in Zimbabwe awarded me the Peace Prize for 2009. In March 2010 I received the US Secretary of State International Women of Courage Award. At the ceremony in the US I was asked to make the acceptance speech for all ten of the women who were honoured – only two of them from Africa. The honour was, for me, the icing on the cake.

During my travels I realised that I represented many people who face injustice, but most of all I saw myself representing the multitude of committed Zimbabweans who were demanding that human rights be respected.

At the beginning of 2010 I accepted an offer of specialised psychological treatment for post-traumatic stress disorder at the Denmar Clinic in Pretoria, South Africa. Takudzwa, who had decided to take a gap year after his A levels (Advanced level examinations) to be with me, joined me in sessions therapy with Dr Steenkamp, which went on for six weeks. During those six weeks he could not hide his joy. 'Mama, I am so happy you are the mother that I know and I am enjoying your cooking that I had gone without for such a long time.'

The ordeal and the events subsequent to it had caused us to drift apart, overwhelmed, at times, by attention from friends and relatives.

During our time in Pretoria we had time to bond and he opened up about his feelings, anxieties and fears during the time that I was away.

On my birthday in March 2011 the French Embassy in Harare announced that I had been awarded the *Légion d'Honneur*, which dates back to Napoleon's time.

Two academic institutions accepted me as a visiting fellow. For five months in 2010 as the recipient of the Oak Fellowship, whose theme that year was incarceration and human rights, I lectured at Colby College in Maine in the USA, sharing my experience with the students.

Takudzwa accompanied me, having been given the opportunity to join students of International Relations as part of his gap year. The idea of this book was conceived at Colby with the help of the Director of the Oak Institute, Professor Walter Hatch.

I organised for several Zimbabweans to visit Colby during my time there, as a way of giving the college community the chance to learn more about Zimbabwe.

Tawanda Mutasa, a Zimbabwean living in the US, presented a paper that was well received by the many Zimbabwean students at Colby who were drawn closer to home. Mbira maestro Chiwoniso Maraire, now sadly deceased, brought the roof down with her music on a day that included introducing the community to Zimbabwean food.

In 2013 the University of York Centre for Applied Human Rights (CAHR) accepted me as a visiting Human Rights Defender. During my stay in York the people I interacted with at the CAHR helped me to confront my pain and anger – which I thought I had put behind me but which were to linger for a long time. When I had been granted bail in March 2009, wanting to forget the ugly episode, I had been determined to burn the 'gifts' I had received from the state – the dress, the panties, the plastic shoes, as well as the night clothes I had been abducted in, but Beatrice had talked me out of that.

Eventually I had tucked the items away in a bag, which I secured at the top and placed in a cupboard. It was only during my stay at York that I realised that in doing so I had temporarily ignored what I felt in the hope that the feelings would go away. All I had actually achieved was to put them on ice for a while, thereby obstructing the healing process.

The Artist in Residence at CAHR, Juliana Mensah, a Ugandan by origin, first pricked the bubble that made it difficult for me to recount the ordeal and helped me reach out for the bag of pain as I unpacked one 'gift' after the other, confronting it in a different way, thus making the bag breathe, so to speak.

The process itself was harrowing, rekindling and making me relive the ordeal. At times I could actually hear the breath of my tormentors. At times I felt uncomfortable as I imagined myself in the corner of the interrogation room. During that time I also remember dreaming I had been abducted again and was relieved to wake up and realise that I was in York. The distance gave me a sense of security.

It was also in York that the seeds of this book, sown in Maine, grew to fruition as I began to write seriously. Until then, the memories of my experience had been too raw. When I got to York it was as though a smokescreen had been removed and, with Juliana Mensah's encouragement, I was able to start to express myself.

During my time in York I visited Minster Acres in Northumberland, a serene place that fits in well with the project of respite. While undertaking the journey of life at Minster Acres I came across a tree known as the elephant tree because, having been damaged in a storm it resembles an elephant. Although significantly transformed from its original form, it has a new form and teaches those who have endured pain to realise that life goes on, even though its form might have been transformed. It is not easy to get back everything that has been lost or damaged in a 'storm'.

I broke down several times and had nightmares and the CAHR put me in touch with a man of the cloth, Reverend Rory Dalgliesh of the Methodist Church. Rev Dalgliesh, a tall, well-built South African, had a unique way of making me not only accept the fact that I harboured a great deal of pain and anger but realise that in time I would be healed.

During one of the sessions he said, 'I want you to realise that not everyone, including your son, wants to be reminded of the dark episode, so approach it with caution. Allow those who do not want to be reminded not to be.' I recognised the truth of this and confirmed that to him. For instance, when I had sent Takudzwa a message asking him to refresh my memory about the names of the dogs we had in 2008 because I felt it was important to recall them, his offhand response had left me bewildered. 'What do you want the names for?' he had asked, irritated.

While there I also had the rare opportunity to meet face to face Val

Norton, one of the many Amnesty International members who had supported me. She had written me a letter of solidarity that had included her address so I had written to update her on the various court cases.

Both the Oak Institute, through Colby College, and the University of York removed me from the frontline and provided an opportunity for respite as well as further research into human rights.

CHAPTER
thirteen ▍Aftermath

I t was not only activists who suffered the wrath of the government; two journalists who dared reveal the names of our abductors were arrested and charged for merely doing their job.

Constantine Chimakure of the *Zimbabwe Independent*, for instance, wrote two articles in the week beginning 8 May 2009. They were headed 'Activists' abductors named' and 'CIO police role in activists' abduction revealed'.

Despite the fact that the information contained in the articles came from public documents, Chimakure and Vincent Kahiya, the man who edited the articles, were arrested in terms of section 31(a) (iii) of the Criminal Law (Codification and Reform Act). This prohibits the publication or communication to any other person of a false statement with the intention of undermining public confidence in the law enforcement agency, the prison service or the defence forces of Zimbabwe or when realising that there is a real risk or possibility of such confidence being undermined. Chimakure had written:

A perusal of the notices revealed that Assistant Director External in the CIO, retired Brigadier Asher Walter Tapfumanei, police superintendents Reggies Chitekwe and Joel Tenderere, detective inspectors Elliot Muchada and Joshua Muzanango, officer commanding CID Homicide Crispen Makedenge, Chief Super-intendent Peter Magwenzi, and Senior Assistant Commissioner Simon Nyathi were involved in some of the abductees' cases.

The journalists took the matter to the Constitutional Court, arguing that the section under which they were charged contravened the fundamental right to freedom of expression contained in section 20(1) of the Constitution.

On 23 July 2014 Deputy Chief Justice Luke Malaba handed down a judgement which upheld the argument of the appellants: 'It is the order of the court that Section 31 (a) (iii) of the Criminal Law (Codification and Reform) Act Chapter 9:23 was in contravention of Section 20(1) of the former Constitution and therefore void.'

In 2013, the ZPP and I were again targeted by the state. The trouble began when police raided the project's offices on 11 February in search of 'any subversive material, documents, gadgets and recording equipment and any illegal immigrants'. They confiscated wind-up radios that had been donated by a sister organisation and were destined for our members. They also confiscated four smartphones, which, like any other smart phone, came fitted with a geographical positioning system (GPS).

The experience of the raid, which took place during a workshop we were holding for monitors, taught me that friends and colleagues could desert you and offer you as a sacrifice in the face of impending risk. I learned that one individual among the staff had proposed that I should be the one to be arrested, advancing the notion that since I had previously been incarcerated and my case had been profiled internationally I would be released in no time.

I failed to understand how someone who purported to work with me at the highest level could wish the worst for me. I say the worst because it is not the idea of being arrested that I fear, if the arrest is justified. What I fear the most are the conditions at the detention centres.

In 2014 Jenny Williams and Magodonga Mahlangu of Women of Zimbabwe Arise challenged the state in the Constitutional Court about the conditions in the holding cells at Harare Central Police Station and the degrading treatment of suspects, especially women, who were forced to remove their undergarments. The court ruled in their favour – a victory for all citizens, especially those who knew about or had suffered this treatment.

The notion that some people are suited to detention centres rekindled the thoughts that occupied me during my incarceration, when individuals I had regarded as friends simply disappeared, making no effort either to visit me in prison or to console my family. Their lack of support briefly resulted in my walking the wrong lane, blaming myself for what was happening to me.

The raid was not the only reminder I had that year that I was still considered an enemy of the state. I was watching the news on television at home on the evening of 7 March when my picture filled the screen and an appeal was made by the Commissioner General of Police to citizens to report to the nearest police station if they saw me. It was the kind of appeal that is put out when hard core criminals are sought by the police.

While I watched with my niece Wilma, her daughters, untouched by the fear that overwhelmed me when my face appeared on state media, they jumped up and down with excitement at seeing me on television. My niece prayed with me, noticing that I was shaking like a reed. The statement was made on the erroneous assumption that I was on the run, although the police had not visited either my office or my home before making it. My mother, who was not watching television at the time but was informed of it by neighbours, suffered a mild stroke.

The next day I reported to the police in the company of Beatrice and Harrison. Four charges were laid against me:
- running an unregistered organisation;
- taking part in the management of an unregistered organisation;

- smuggling radios and mobile phones; and
- in line with the Broadcasting Services Act failing or refusing to register as a dealer.

I signed a warned and cautioned statement and was released into the custody of my lawyers. I was further perplexed when I continuously appeared on a hit list publicised on the social media platform, Facebook, by a shadowy figure, 'Baba Jukwa', who boasted of knowing the plans being hatched by Zanu-PF.

As though this was not enough for a single individual to deal with, when my passport needed to be renewed I approached, as I always had, people that I knew at the Registrar General's office, including a relative, as a way of avoiding the long, winding queues.

None of them was willing to assist. With no other option I joined the queue on a cold June day. At the end of the day, just as I was ready to leave my forms and go home to wait for my passport to be issued, the woman at the last desk looked up at me from behind her machine and exclaimed, 'Aah!' She looked at me again and her expression told me something was wrong. She pulled out a red pen, wrote 'SL' on the right-hand corner of the form, and instructed me to 'Go to office number 7'. I tried to ask why, but the woman was already signalling to the next applicant. I held the application form to my eyes as if expecting an explanation for 'SL' to pop out. In office number 7 the officials were busy and all the chairs were occupied. One of the officials barked at three of us who were standing in the middle of the room, ordering us to leave until the other people in the room had been attended to. Realising that it was almost closing time, I reluctantly retreated to the door.

I kept peering around the door and eventually caught the attention of one of the officials, who signalled that I should go in. After looking at my form he announced that I must return in three days when my papers had been examined to establish why I was on the 'Stop List'. I had never heard of a 'Stop List' and there was no time to ask what it was, the official was already attending to someone else.

Confused, I called one of my lawyer friends, who told me that the list

110

contained the names of those who were banned from receiving travel documents. She said it was against the law for the Registrar's department to place citizens on a 'Stop List'. She advised me to wait for the three days and insisted that Zimbabwe Lawyers for Human Rights would arrange for a lawyer to accompany me when I returned. I have since learned that I was not the only one on the Stop List – the names of other abductees such as Emmanuel Chinazvavana, *sekuru* Chiramba and Violet were on it too. This means that the list had something to do with the 2008 abductions and the spurious charges brought against us. Surprisingly, I was issued a passport in 2010 with no mention of a Stop List.

I reached home overcome by emotion and the overwhelming feeling that the walls were caving in on my head.

Not knowing what to expect, I was accompanied to the Registrar General's office by Dr Tarisai Mutangi and, as I walked into office 7, the man who accepted my form smiled. 'Everything is fine, my sister, you can now go and submit your form.' My attempts to get an explanation were to no avail. 'But why was I on the list?' I asked. 'My sister, there are too many people here. I have just said everything is fine. I will take you to the other side so that you do not queue.'

These events took place a few months before the watershed elections in Zimbabwe, intended to determine who would take over the reins of power as both Zanu-PF and Tsvangirai's MDC were uneasy about operating in the coalition government. I had a rare opportunity to speak to then Youth Minister, Saviour Kasukuwere of Zanu-PF, who laid the problem bare. 'Being in this government is like wearing the right shoe on the left foot and vice versa. You can walk but it is extremely uncomfortable.'

The ZPP was not the only civil society organisation to be targeted during that difficult period – a wave of office raids affected a number of other organisations. Many people predicted increasing violence as the date of the election drew near. They were right, but the forms of violence were different from those that had preceded other elections. There was a significant reduction in gross acts of physical violence but they were replaced by harassment and intimidation, with citizens being reminded of the violence in the run-up to the June 2008 presidential run-off if they dared make the wrong choices. An example could be seen on election day, when huge numbers of people had to be 'assisted' to vote, in a country with high literacy rates.

The work I was doing and continue to do does not contravene any of the country's laws and I am determined to continue amplifying the voices of those who face any form of injustice. I do not know what the future holds for my country, of which I am so proud. I had hoped and prayed that, with the new Constitution, which came into force on 22 May 2013, the country would adopt a culture of respecting the rights of citizens and ensuring that they are granted the dignity guaranteed in the Bill of Rights. Sadly, at the time of writing, my hopes have not been answered. Even though I had made tremendous progress towards healing I realised that the process would be long and expensive. It just takes the anniversary of the abduction for the pain and anguish to be rekindled. Even as I wrote this book some sections brought tears and nightmares.

I have not emerged from the experience the same person – I lived the experience that I had heard about so often through my work with the ZPP and that has changed the way that I look at things. It is no longer just figures and the testimonies of X, Y, and Z.

At a spiritual level, the experience has re-energised and boosted my faith. My scars have a covering but they are still visible and will remain a constant reminder of the dark episode that changed my life forever. However, I still need to work hard to heal them completely and that is a different and intense process. Although at one point I was keen to meet my tormentors, I did not know what I would have done if that had happened in those early months, when the memories were vivid and the pain was still very fresh.

Following up on the fate of other 2008 abductees I realise that their experiences are still very fresh, to the extent that they still feel the pain. Almost all of them speak continually of losses they suffered as a result of being targeted by the state. *Sekuru* Chiramba lost a plot of land he had, while projects in which Chinazvavana and Mutemagawu were involved and that had contributed to their livelihood, have subsequently crumbled. The tentacles of the experiences of all the detainees have taken hold of their families in ways that have had permanent effects. For the Mutemagawu family, for instance, the greatest scar left by the dark episode is the fact that some of their relatives have ceased to associate with them. They spoke painfully about how they are hardly visited.

The perpetrators have been protected, but I still believe that, if I am to heal completely, I deserve to know the truth about why I was abducted. In the words of UN Secretary General Ban Ki-Moon:

> The right to the truth is both an individual and a collective right. Each victim has the right to know the truth about violations against them, but the truth also has to be told more widely as a safeguard to prevent violations from happening again.